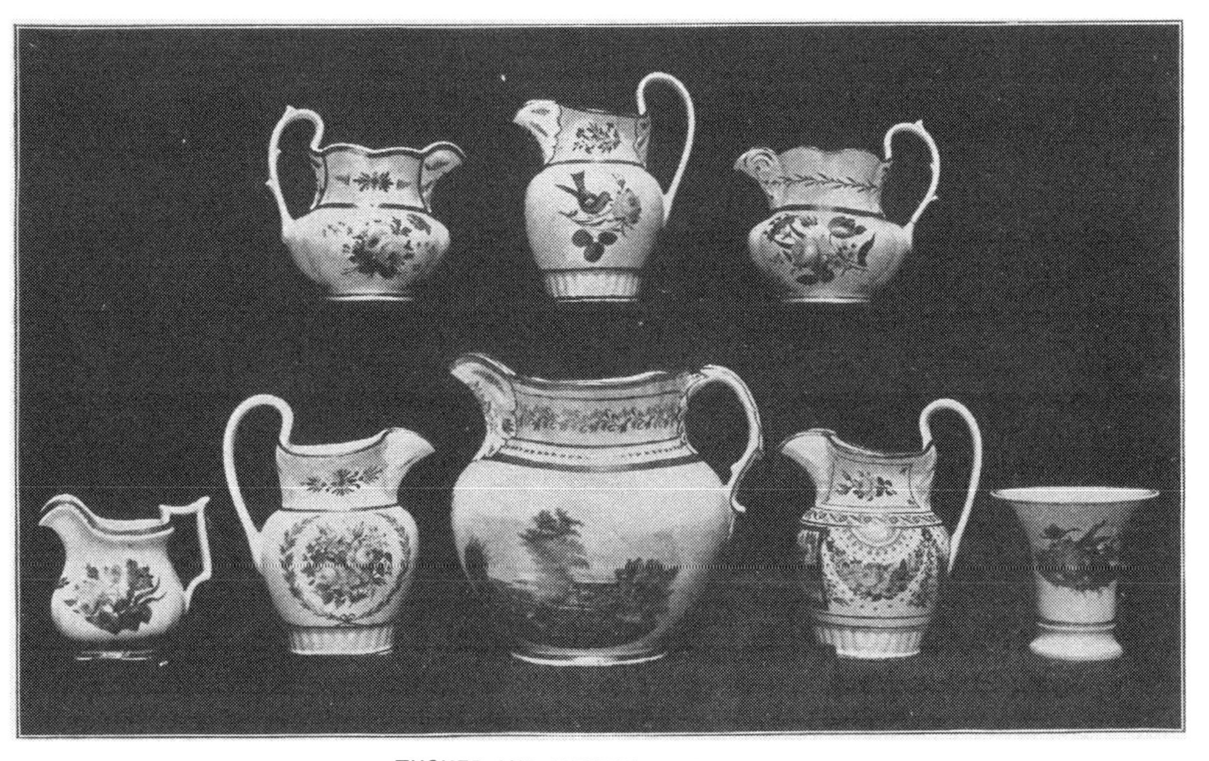

TUCKER AND HEMPHILL PORCELAIN.
*Made in Philadelphia*, 1828–1835.
In the Pennsylvania Museum, Philadelphia.

# MARKS

OF

# AMERICAN POTTERS

BY

EDWIN ATLEE BARBER, A.M., PH.D.,

*Curator and Secretary of the Pennsylvania Museum and School of Industrial Art.*

*Author of "Pottery and Porcelain of the United States"; "Anglo-American Pottery"; "American Glassware, Old and New"; "Tulip Ware of the Pennsylvania-German Potters," Etc.*

---

WITH FACSIMILES OF 1000 MARKS, AND ILLUSTRATIONS OF RARE EXAMPLES OF AMERICAN WARES.

---

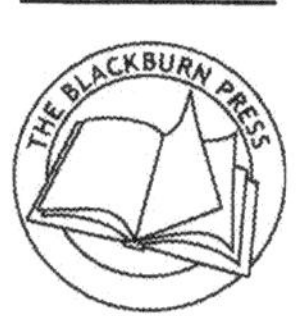

Reprint of First Edition, Copyright 1904



Marks of American Potters

ISBN-10: 1-930665-41-5
ISBN-13: 978-1-930665-41-5

Library of Congress Control Number: 2001093231

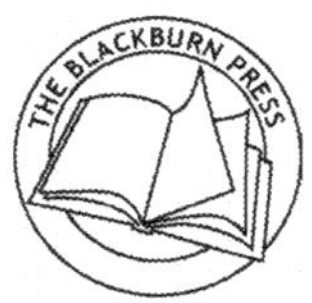


**THE BLACKBURN PRESS**
P. O. Box 287
Caldwell, New Jersey 07006 U.S.A.
973-228-7077
www.BlackburnPress.com

# Preface.

THE first attempt to figure the marks of American potters was made by the author in his *Pottery and Porcelain of the United States,* in 1893, in which less than one hundred varieties, found principally on the earlier wares, were shown. Previous to that time none of the manuals on potters' marks contained any reference to the ceramic products of this country.

The scope of this work, as originally planned, has been extended to include the principal marks, whether those of factories, patterns, workmen or decorators, which have been used in America down to the present day, on both artistic and commercial wares, for the double purpose of enabling collectors to recognize and identify examples which possess historical value, and to furnish users of modern household china with information which may be utilized in renewing or completing desired patterns. The majority of the cuts of marks here used first appeared in connection with a series of articles by the present writer in the *China, Glass and Pottery Review,* and some of the full-page illustrations, which were first published in *Old China,* are reproduced through the courtesy of the publisher of that magazine.

The earlier marks shown in these pages, and many of the later ones, have been copied from examples of ware in the unique collection of American Pottery and Porcelain in the Pennsylvania Museum, Memorial Hall, Philadelphia.

E. A. B.

October, 1904.

# CONTENTS.

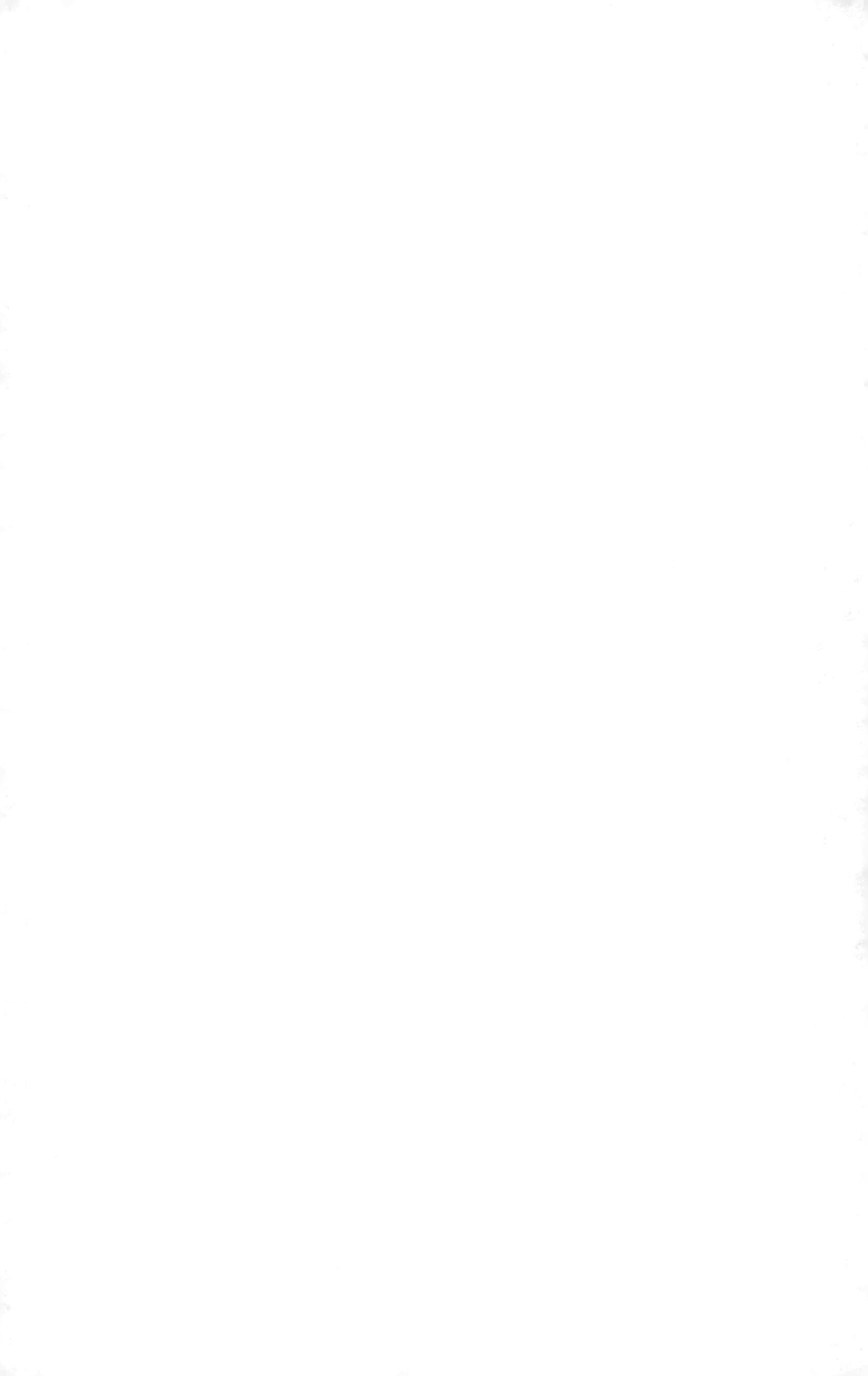

# ILLUSTRATIONS.

# PENNSYLVANIA POTTERIES

# PENNSYLVANIA.

## BONNIN & MORRIS, PHILADELPHIA.

THE earliest mark of any kind that has yet been discovered on American pottery or porcelain occurs on a small cream-ware fruit dish or openwork basket, with relief rosettes and painted blue decorations beneath the glaze, which was made at the china factory of Bonnin & Morris, in Southwark, Philadelphia, about the year 1770. It is simply a capital letter P, *penciled or painted in dark blue color under the glaze.* It is not known whether this character was intended to indicate Philadelphia, the place of manufacture, or was the initial of the name of the painter of the floral device which ornaments the interior of the dish. It is probable that it was a factory mark, employed by the proprietors to distin-

**P**

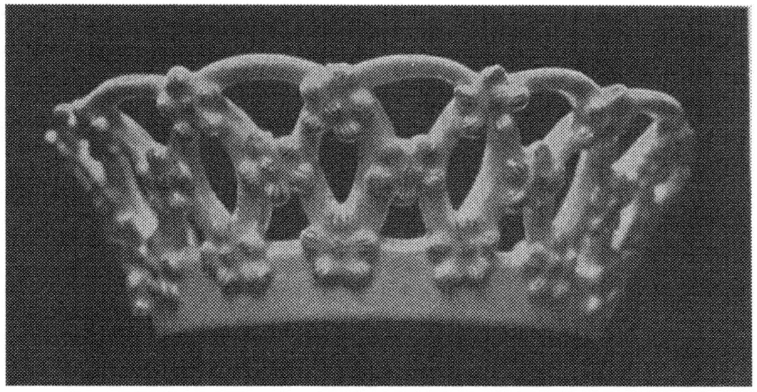

1. Cream-ware Fruit Basket; Blue Decorations, Underglaze.
Bonnin & Morris, Southwark, Philadelphia, 1770. In the Pennsylvania Museum.

guish their ware from similar designs of that period, which were being produced at Bow and Worcester, England. This dish, which is the only known piece from this early factory, has been deposited in the Pennsylvania Museum by the Franklin Institute.

---

## PENNSYLVANIA-GERMAN POTTERIES.

The old German potters of Eastern Pennsylvania, who made slip-decorated and sgraffito earthenware from about 1730 to 1850, used but few marks.* Some of their more recent wares are stamped with a circular mark containing relief figures, which indicate the sizes or shapes of the vessels. At the Joseph Smith Pottery, in Bucks County, Pa., pieces were frequently marked, from about 1767 to the beginning of the last century, with the date of manufacture and the name of the maker. One of these marks occurs on a black glazed pottery barrel-shaped water vessel of large size. It was scratched in the clay before it was burned.

Other Pennsylvania-German potters used similar marks. Henry Roudebush made ornamental pie plates in Montgomery County, Pa., on which his name is occasionally found. Examples that are known bear dates ranging from 1811 to 1816. In some instances his initials alone appear.

Samuel Troxel, of the same county, also made sgraffito earthenware of a highly decorative character, which usually bore his name and dates from about 1823 to 1833. Occasionally his initials are found on the backs of plates, scratched in the clay.

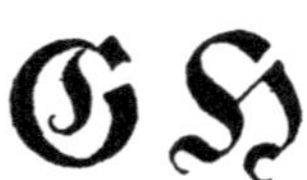

Georg Hübener was another Pennsylvania-German potter who had an establishment in the same county between 1785 and 1798. He made earthenware decorated in the sgraffito style, with figures of peacocks, tulips and other motives and inscriptions with the dates of manufacture. Occasionally his name appears in full on large, circular dishes, and one

* See "Tulip Ware of the Pennsylvania-German Potters." Published as an Art Handbook by the Pennsylvania Museum.

example in the Museum collection bears his initials, carved in old German text.

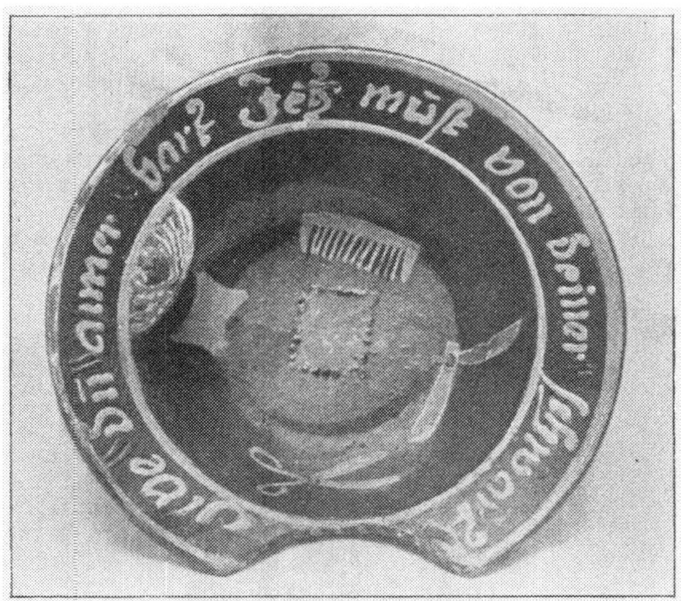

2. Slip-Decorated Shaving Basin. Pennsylvania-German, about 1750.
In the Pennsylvania Museum.
Inscription: Sive (*siebe*) du armer bart
Jetz must von deiner schwart.
Translation: (I must) lather you, poor beard,
Now (you) must (come) from your hide.

The letters I. T. which are found on molded red pottery dishes of octagonal form, with relief ornamentation, are supposed to be the initials of Jacob or Isaac Taney who operated a pottery in Bucks Co., Pa. Several of these have come to light, all bearing the date 1794.

IT

A pie plate with tulip decoration, in the collection of Prof. John M. Clarke, of Albany, N. Y., is marked with the name

Johan Drey 1809

of Johan Drey, who is believed to have been a potter in Eastern Pennsylvania in 1809.

AH

Andrew Headman, whose pottery was situated at Rock Hill, Bucks Co., Pa., in 1808, used the initials of his name to mark his wares. Examples of sgraffito ware may be seen in the collection of the Bucks County Historical Society of Doylestown, Pa., and the Pennsylvania Museum bearing this mark and date.

PVM

Johannes Neesz, David Spinner, Heinrich Stofflet, Philip Kline, Rudolf Drach, Conrad K. Ranninger and Abraham Weaver were other potters in the same district who sometimes signed their productions.

H.T. IS.T.

Other marks found on Pennsylvania-German pottery, which have not been identified, are P. V. M. and H. T. IS. T.

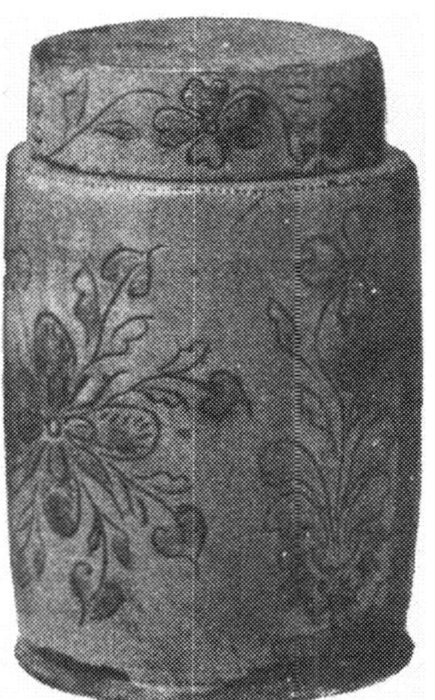

3. Sgraffito Jar. By Jacob Scholl, Montgomery Co., Pa., about 1830. In the Pennsylvania Museum.

Jacob Scholl, of Tyler's Port, Montgomery County, Pa., produced the same class of ware about 1830. He occasionally used the mark of a conventionalized *fuchsia,* a favorite flower with the Pennsylvania Germans. This was *impressed* in the wet clay with an engraved or modeled stamp. Several pieces bearing this device have come to light, the impression being an inch in size.

## WOMELSDORF, PA.

An earthenware pottery was established in Berks County, Pa., at Womelsdorf, by John Menner, in 1784, which later passed into the hands of Josiah Beck, and in 1864 was bought by the present owner, Willoughby Smith. Ordinary red, slip-decorated ware has been made here for perhaps nearly a century, such as pie plates, flower-pots, apple butter and milk jars. A mark used by Mr. Smith on some of his earlier ware consists of his name and address, impressed in the ware with type or a metal die.

**Willoughby Smith**
**Wumelsdorf**

At present machine-made flower-pots are a specialty at this pottery.

## THOMAS AND JOHN VICKERS, DOWNINGTOWN, PA.

Thomas Vickers established a pottery near Downingtown, Pa., previous to the year 1806. One of his day books, extending over a period from this date to 1813, has been preserved, and from the entries we learn that he produced at various times red earthenware, sgraffito ware, black glazed pottery, "domestic queensware" and green enameled ware. Among the articles enumerated are pie plates, milk pots, "basons," jugs, pitchers, bowls, mugs, cups, coffee and tea pots, sugar bowls, cream cups, "salt cups," "bouquetts," cake molds, candlesticks, "salt sellers," mantel and toy figures, chimney ornaments, bread baskets, chimney stands, inkstands, dishes, plates and tobacco pipes, both glazed and unglazed. There are numerous entries of green enameled ware, such as pint, quart and three-pint pitchers, sugar bowls, etc. In the

Museum collection is a large jar with incised decorations,—a wreath on one side enclosing the words "Apple Butter," and on the other the name of the recipient and the date 1807. The entire surface is covered with a beautiful, mottled, apple-green enamel. Other examples in the collection, from this pottery, are a sgraffito decorated flower pot, bearing the date 1826, and a spherical jar with variegated glaze and date 1822.

Thomas Vickers took his son, John, into partnership, under the firm name of Thomas Vickers & Son. In 1822 the pottery was moved to Lionville, Pa., and the style became John Vickers & Son. Pieces of pottery have been found bearing the incised initials T. V., also J. V. The latter occur on some pottery pie-plate molds in this Museum, accompanied by dates ranging from 1806 to 1828.

---

## AMERICAN CHINA MANUFACTORY, PHILADELPHIA.

William Ellis Tucker
China Manufacturer
Philadelphia
1828

Tucker & Hulme
China Manufacturers
Philadelphia
1828

Tucker & Hulme.
Philadelphia
1828

Manufactured
by Jos. Hemphill
Philad.

W

Hard porcelain was produced by William Ellis Tucker, in Philadelphia, as early as 1825. The first mark used was his name and address *painted on the glaze in black*. A vase-shaped pitcher bears this mark with the date 1828. In the latter year he took into partnership Thomas Hulme. The ware was of a superior quality, and the overglaze decorations were painted in colors by hand. Many of the designs were exceedingly artistic. The mark, *penciled in red,* consisted of the firm name and the date of production. Two varieties of this mark, which was only used during the year named, are known, reduced facsimiles of which are here shown. (See illustration 4.)

In 1832 Judge Joseph Hemphill entered into partnership with Mr. Tucker, who died in the same year. Judge Hemphill continued the manufacture until about 1836. His mark, occasionally found, was similar to the preceding.

Private marks of workmen are often found *impressed* in Tucker and Hemphill porcelain. A capital W, either in script or straight lines, was used, to a considerable extent, by Andrew Craig Walker, one of the foremost molders of the factory. It occurs on many of the best pieces.

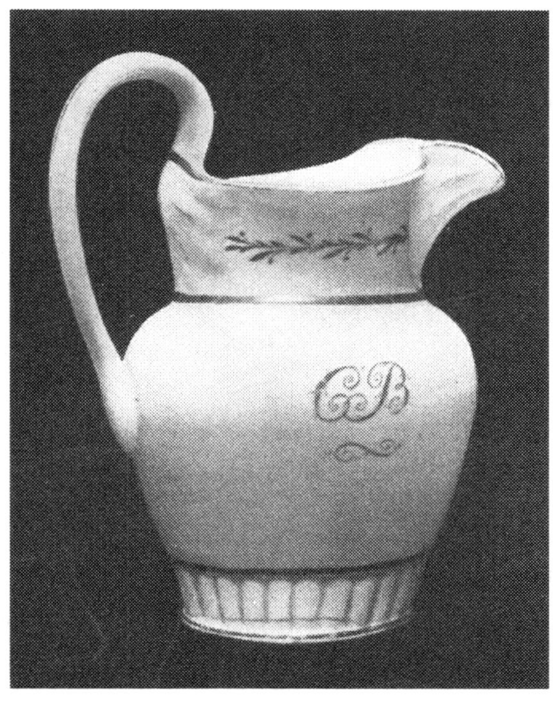

4. **Hard Porcelain Pitcher.** Gold Decorations.
**Tucker and Hulme, Philadelphia, 1828.**
**In the Pennsylvania** Museum.

Joseph Morgan, another molder, used a small written *m*, and occasionally a capital M.

Charles Frederick, also a molder, connected with the same works, scratched his initial in the paste, a capital F, in script.

H

V

CB

A capital H was the private mark of William Hand, an employe of the Philadelphia pottery.

One Vivian, a Frenchman, marked his work with a capital V.

A monogram, composed of the letters C and B, which is sometimes found on Tucker and Hemphill pieces, is supposed to have been the private mark of Charles J. Boulter, who, for a while, was connected with this establishment, and afterward became foreman at the pottery of Abraham Miller, in the same city. A capital B, sometimes seen, may also have been employed by him.

Other initials of workmen occur on the Tucker and Hemphill ware, but it is difficult at this late day to identify them.

The following letter, written by Mr. Tucker to a United States Senator in 1831, now printed for the first time, will convey some idea of the condition of the porcelain industry in this country at that period:

Philada January 31st 1831

Genl Bernard

Dear Sir

I observe that *China* or *Porcelain* has been enumerated in the list of articles brought before the Senate by Mr. Smith of Maryland for the purpose of effecting a *reduction of duty.* Permit me to embrace the present opportunity to state that such a measure would completely destroy my business and crush my establishment for the manufacture of American Porcelain; at a period too, when it particularly calls for the fostering hand of Congress to protect it from the premeditated assaults of European Establishments.

I have sent samples of my ware to various parts of the world; and, last Session, to President Jackson, and have sold large quantities of the article throughout the United States; and you may see by the following extract taken from Poulsons daily advertiser of the 24 of Jan 1831 the estimation in which this Article is held abroad. "Extract of a letter written by an American Gentleman in Paris to his friend in Chester County dated Paris October 29th 1830: 'Within the last four weeks I have made several excursions to the Country to St. Dennis Montmorency Sevres & Co. The latter place is famed for its *porcelain Manufacture,* the first in the World..... I am too near the end of my letter to enter into a description of that interesting place, but what is worthy of particular note is, that among the Specimens of Porcelain *from all parts of the Globe that from Philada* is *ranked second* to the French, *which is first.* All that is wanting in Tuckers manufactory to make the article *equal,* if *not superior,* is the Moulding' "......

There are ample quantities of the Material existing in this Country of a superior quality for the manufacture of Porcelain upon a large Scale. This circumstance connected with the admitted perfection to which I have brought the art, would render it highly impolitic as well as unjust for Congress to remove the duty which is now too small to give that protection which the business requires; I will therefore feel deeply indebted, for your kind exertions to have Porcelain *Struck off* from the above mentioned list....... I suffer materially from the duplicity of the French Manufacturers They are continually in the habit of shipping Porcelain to New York under a false invoice below the real value of the article and by this means evade a part of the duty..But this is an evil I do not see how to remove..................

I have thought, at some suitable time, to make a proposition to Congress, that if they would give me Forty thousand Dollars to enable me to put up a handsome Manufactory & to increase my business I would convey to the United States a complete description of the difficult art of making Porcelain, so as to secure for ever, the benefits of the discovery to our country; and by this means enable her to increase at pleasure the number of manufacturing establishments. I will leave you to judge whether there is an opening for such a proposal this session. I have sent a copy of this letter to each of the representatives of the City of Phila. & to the two members of the Senate

With sentiments of true respect I am
your obedient servant

Wm Ellis Tucker

The Tucker and Hemphill porcelain, as has already been stated, is hard paste, only a very small percentage of bone entering into its composition. In appearance it strongly resembles the French hard porcelain of the same period, but may usually be distinguished from the latter by its bluish tint, which is particularly noticeable in those places where the glaze has accumulated in glass-like deposits. The French ware is generally smoother and more carefully potted than the American, which latter is frequently uneven or less true in outline. On the other hand, the bright gold used on the Philadelphia ware is heavier and of a better quality than that of the average French product, although never variegated with dull gold ornamentation on the burnished gilding, like that seen on some of the more elaborate pieces of the imported ware. It is safe to assume that every piece so decorated is of European origin.

In the painting of flowers, in natural colors, the decorators connected with the Philadelphia establishment fully equaled the French painters, but their work in landscape or figure painting, as seen in the panels of vases, was inferior.

Messrs. Tucker and Hemphill closely imitated many of the forms of French pieces, notably several styles of vases, thus increasing the resemblance between the two products, but a number of shapes originated at this factory which may always be recognized, such as the "vase-shaped" pitcher shown in illustration 4, with its cylindrical body, tall arching handle and fluted base. This shape was designed at the Philadelphia works, and is not known to have been produced at any other factory.

Both the French and the American hard porcelain were frequently, but not always, marked with initials or figures scratched in the paste, which were the private marks of workmen or the numbers of sizes or shapes. Those copied above are seldom, if ever, found on the foreign ware. The W occurs more frequently on the Tucker ware than any of the other letters, and is usually a trustworthy indication that the piece which bears it was modeled or molded by Andrew Walker of the Tucker factory.

It will thus be seen that in some instances identification, by means of color of body or glaze, form, goldwork or marks, is a matter of considerable ease, while in others, where forms are similar and the differentiation in other respects is slight, no rules can be given that will enable the uninitiated to positively distinguish the American from the French product. In such cases the investigator will do well to apply to an expert, or refer to the original pattern books of the Tucker and Hemphill factory, which are preserved in the Pennsylvania Museum.

---

## SMITH, FIFE & CO., PHILADELPHIA.

The firm of Smith, Fife & Co. exhibited "two beautiful porcelain pitchers" at the annual exhibition of the Franklin

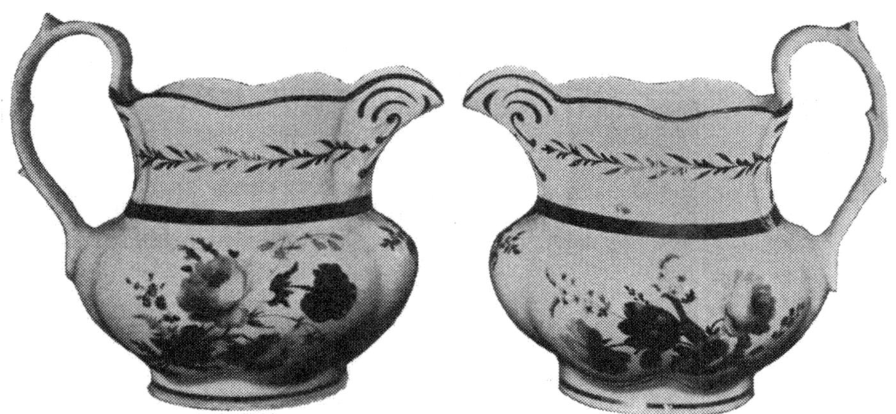

5. Porcelain Pitchers. Decorations in Colors, Overglaze. Smith, Fife & Co., Philadelphia, 1830.

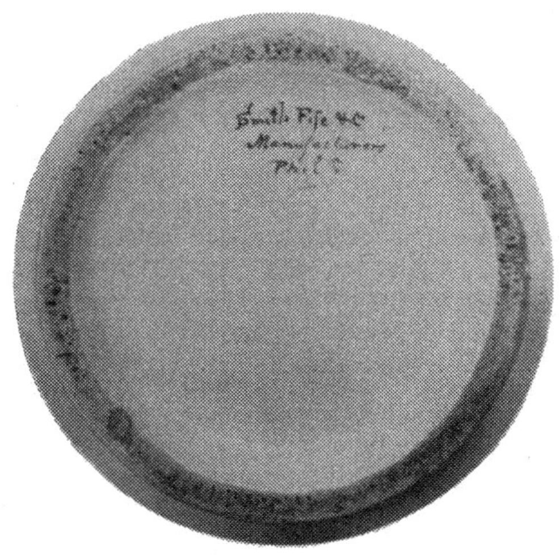

6. Base of Pitcher, showing Mark.

Institute, Philadelphia, in 1830. The manufacture does not appear to have continued for any length of time, since no other reference to this firm occurs in the annual reports of these exhibitions. Two fine examples of their ware, bearing the mark "Smith, Fife & Co., Manufacturers, Phila.," penciled in red, are owned by a lady in New Hampshire (see illustration 5). In form they resemble the "Grecian" pattern of pitcher made by William Ellis Tucker, of Philadelphia, in the same year, as figured in "Pottery and Porcelain of the United States." The decorations are also similar, being well-painted floral designs in natural colors, with heavy gilding.

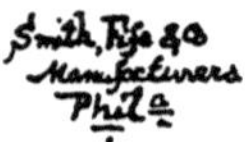

It is said that Mr. Jason Fennemore, a merchant and accountant of Philadelphia, had a financial interest in the enterprise. This partner sent the two pitchers, to which reference has been made, and which are here figured, to an aunt of the present owner, together with two pickle dishes of leaf shape, a smelling bottle and a small heart-shaped ornament or vinaigrette, for the neck, all of the same ware and similarly decorated. The decorative treatment, the heavy goldwork and the shapes of the pieces which have come to light strongly suggest the Tucker hard porcelain of the same period. A careful examination, however, reveals the fact that the Smith, Fife & Co. ware lacks the bluish tinge of the Tucker porcelain, being of a pronounced yellowish-white tone. The coloring and execution of the decorations are also somewhat inferior. One of the pickle dishes, referred to above, has recently been added to the Museum collection, and proves to be of identical pattern and size with two examples in the same collection from the Tucker factory. The simultaneous use of the same shapes by the two establishments appears at first to be a puzzling coincidence, which, however, may be explained by the supposition that the modeler supplied the molds to both potteries which, in 1830, were the only ones in Philadelphia where porcelain was produced. It was usual at that period for professional designers and modelers, who were not attached to any particular pottery, to sell their work to more than one establishment, hence the same designs are often found among the products of several manufactories which can be distinguished only by peculiarities of body, glaze or decoration. The ware of Smith, Fife & Co., while it may be classed as hard paste, apparently contains a larger proportion of bone than does the Tucker porcelain, and there may be other variations in composition, which would account for the perceptible difference in color. It would seem that the venture was financially unsuccessful.

---

## RALPH BAGNALL BEECH, PHILADELPHIA, PA.

Ralph Bagnall Beech was born in London, England, in 1810, and in his youth entered the Wedgwood pottery, at Etruria, where he learned the business in all of its details.

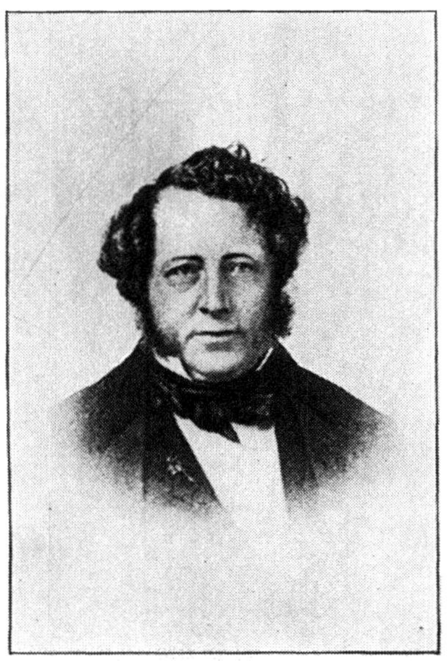

7. Portrait of Ralph Bagnall Beech, Potter.
Born, 1810. Died, 1857.

On attaining his majority he entered into business on his own account, but, after a time, deciding to come to the United States, he sold his interests and arrived in Philadelphia in

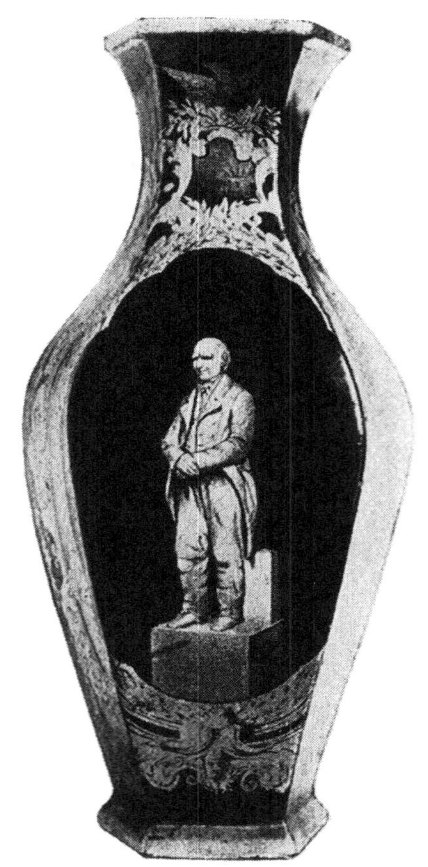

8. Stephen Girard Vase.
Japanned and Painted Earthenware.
By Ralph B. Beech, Kensington, Philadelphia, 1851.
In the Pennsylvania Museum.

1842. At first he worked in the pottery of Abraham Miller, and in 1845 he established a pottery of his own in Kensington, Philadelphia. He took out several patents, among which was one for "ornamenting baked earthenware," which was issued on June 3, 1851 (see patent No. 8140, Patent Office Reports). His process consisted in the inlaying of mother-of-pearl in the surface of the white biscuit ware, and filling the spaces between with black or blue enamel. A tall six-sided vase in the Pennsylvania Museum, covered with a black ground, on the front panel of which is a full-length figure of Stephen Girard, painted in white, surrounded by heavy gilt scroll-work, bears the impressed mark here shown (see illustration 8).

**RALPH B. BEECH**
**PATENTED**
**JUNE 3, 1851**
**KENSINGTON, PA.**

Two vases of similar form, in possession of his daughter, Mrs. George B. Lukens, are richly ornamented with clusters of fruit and flowers inlaid in mother-of-pearl. The ground is black enamel, filled to the surface of the pearl and rubbed smooth.

The first pieces of this ware were enameled for Mr. Beech by D. D. Dick, a japanner, whose place was in St. James Street (now Commerce), below Seventh. In 1851 Mr. Beech exhibited at the Franklin Institute a lot of porcelain flower and scent vases and some examples of japanning on earthenware, the decorations of which were beautifully executed.

The writer has been informed that a number of portraits of prominent men were painted on vases, including one of John Price Wetherill, a well-known Philadelphian. These were the work of William Crombie, from Edinburgh, Scotland, who was also an excellent painter of landscapes and floral designs.

We have also seen pitchers in brown glaze modeled to represent the head of Daniel O'Connell, the Irish patriot, produced at the Beech pottery about 1848. One of these, unmarked, is in the Pennsylvania Museum collection. A covered soap dish in mottled Rockingham glaze, bearing the above impressed mark, is in possession of a Trenton collector.

Mr. Beech closed his pottery about 1857, and soon after sailed for Honduras, in the interest of the Honduras Inter-Oceanic Railway, in which country he died of yellow fever within a few weeks of his arrival.

## KURLBAUM & SCHWARTZ, PHILADELPHIA.

In 1851 experiments in the manufacture of hard porcelain were commenced in Kensington, Philadelphia, by Charles Kurlbaum and John T. Schwartz, chemists. In 1853, at the Exhibition of the Franklin Institute, this firm submitted some ware which in the annual report for that year was described by the judges as "the best American porcelain we have ever seen. The body is particularly vitreous and in this respect equal to the best French." This ware, so highly spoken of,

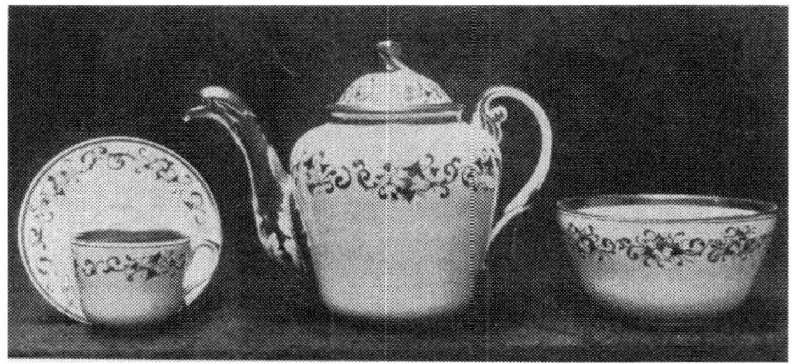

9. **Hard Porcelain Tea Set. Gold Decorations.
By Kurlbaum & Schwartz, Philadelphia, 1853.
In the Pennsylvania Museum.**

was not known to collectors until very recently, when a few pieces were obtained for the Pennsylvania Museum from a son of one of the manufacturers, Mr. Chas. A. Kurlbaum. The following description is taken from a paper prepared by the present writer for *Old China:*

"These pieces consist of a tea pot, bowl and four cups and saucers, the latter of which bear the impressed mark or initials of the manufacturers. The ware itself is a true, hard porcelain, resembling the best French china of the same period. The decorations are in gold, and consist of wreaths of ivy leaves and scroll work. The tea pot is surmounted with a lid on which is a modeled pear, serving as a knob, which is solidly gilded, as is also the spout. Heavy bands of the best quality of gilding extend around the edges of the cups and half an inch down inside (see illustration 9).

K& S

"A small pottery and kilns were erected on Front Street above Jefferson, in Kensington. Mr. Schwartz became acquainted with a German named Reese, who had a pottery in Wilmington, Del., and he was secured to take charge of the new venture. A considerable amount of ware was made during the short time the factory was in operation, but the business never grew to any great proportions. The kaolin for the manufacture of the ware was obtained from Chester County, Pa.

"In the Philadelphia city directory for 1855 will be found the firm name of Kurlbaum & Schwartz, manufacturers of porcelain, at Front below Oxford Street. This appears to have been the year when the manufacture ceased. The venture was not a commercial or financial success, although the ware was undoubtedly the finest porcelain which had ever been produced in this country to that time.

"Mr. Reese afterwards went to Gloucester, N. J. and became interested in the American Porcelain Manufacturing Co., of that place, which was closed in 1857 or 1858.

"The ware made at Gloucester, however, judging from the pieces which have been secured by this Museum, was greatly inferior to the Kurlbaum & Schwartz porcelain, in body, in workmanship and in decorative treatment."

It is said that expert china painters and gilders were brought to Philadelphia from Germany by the Kensington firm. A mark found on one of the pieces described above resembles the letter T, scratched in the paste, and was probably the initial of one of the decorators or workmen.

---

## GEORGE ALLEN, PHILADELPHIA.

Mr. George Allen had a pottery at the corner of Amber and Frankford Road in 1857 and 1858. This pottery was previously occupied by Ralph B. Beech, and after Mr. Allen discontinued the business, the plant was occupied for a time by Richard C. Remmey, for the manufacture of stoneware.

Mr. Allen manufactured white ware, yellow ware, Rockingham ware and, to a limited extent, Parian. Many of his molds used for the cheaper grades of ware were brought from England, but those used in the manufacture of Parian and porcelain were obtained from the Gloucester, N. J., pottery, which was closed about that period.

Mr. Allen claims to have been the first potter, in this country, to erect an improved kiln on the English style.

---

## PHŒNIXVILLE, PA.

Phoenix POttery

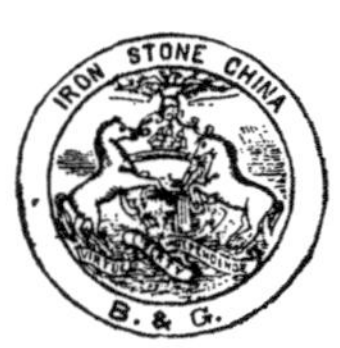


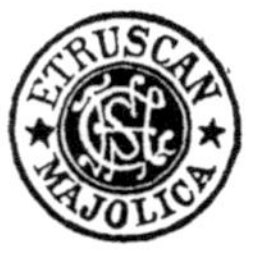

ETRUSCAN

The Phœnix Pottery, Kaolin and Fire Brick Co. was organized at Phœnixville, Pa., on May 7, 1867. The first products were fire brick, yellow and Rockingham wares. In 1872 the works were leased by W. A. H. Schreiber and J. F. Betz. Animal heads in terra-cotta were produced for wall decoration, and the manufacture of Parian was commenced. Lithophanes or transparencies for windows and lamp shades were made to some extent. These were marked with the words "Phœnix Pottery." On January 1, 1877, the pottery was leased to L. B. Beerbower and Henry R. Griffen, the partnership continuing for two years, during which period white granite ware was manufactured, the mark being the Arms of the State of Pennsylvania, with the initials of the firm beneath. In 1879 the style became Griffen, Smith & Hill. In the following year the manufacture of "Etruscan Majolica" was begun. This was stamped with an impressed mark composed of the monogram G. S. H., surrounded by the name of the ware (see illustration 10). Another mark was the monogram alone. The words "Etruscan" and "Etruscan Majolica" were also used occasionally, impressed in the ware. On the uncolored ware they also used the circular Etruscan mark with the word "Ivory" substituted for "Majolica."

In addition to these factory marks, there were usually other marks impressed in the ware, and as these are occasionally found alone they are given here to facilitate identification of the Phœnixville products. These supplementary marks consist of letters and figures, the former indicating the shape of the piece and the latter the style of decoration. The letters run from A to O, as follows:

**ETRUSCAN MAJOLICA**

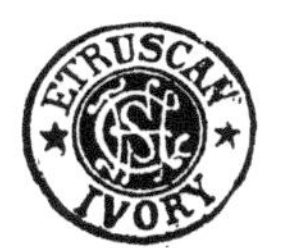


| | | | | |
|---|---|---|---|---|
| A1 | B13 | C4 | D15 | E14 |
| F11 | G2 | H9 | I3 | J10 |
| K8 | L6 | M5 | N7 | O12 |

A1, A2, etc., occur on individual butter plates, round, leaf or flower shape.

B1, B2, etc., on pickle dishes, usually of irregular leaf shape.

C1, C2, etc., on cake trays or dishes, of leaf or flower shape, irregular or round.

D1, D2, etc., on plates of various patterns, round, conventionalized leaf or shell shape.

E1, E2, etc., on hollow vessels, such as pitchers, coffee and tea pots, syrup jugs, sugar and slop bowls.

F1, F2, etc., on cuspidors and jardinières.

G1, G2, etc., on cake baskets.

H1, H2, etc., on bonbon dishes, deep and oval.

I1, I2, etc., on covered boxes.

J1, J2, etc., on comports with pedestals or stands.

K1, K2, etc., on paper weights, pin trays or small flower jars, and occasionally cheese dishes and trays of special form.

L1, L2, etc., on celery vases, mugs, pepper and salt shakers, jewel trays and comports with dolphin-shaped feet.

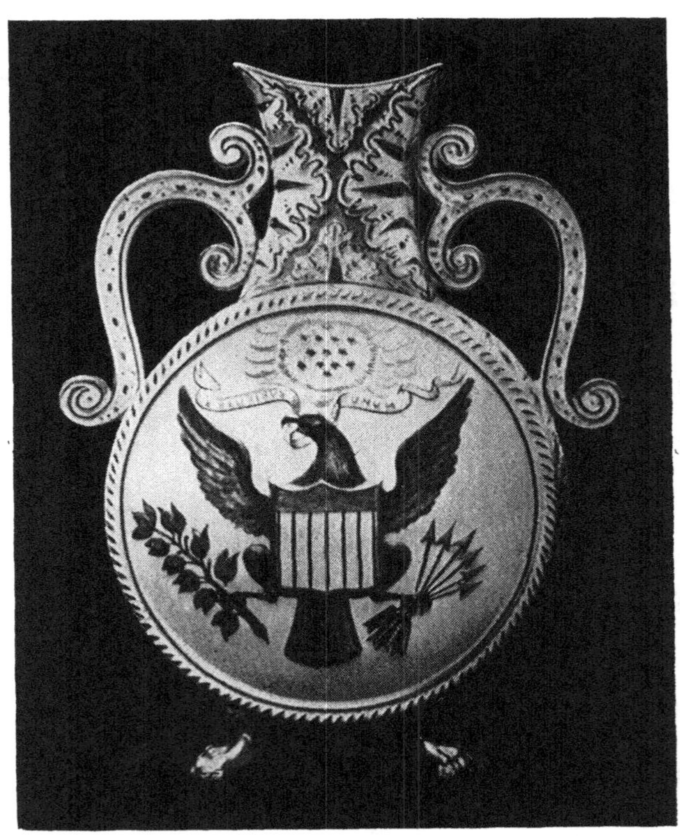

10. Majolica Vase. Arms of the United States in Colors and Gold.
**Phœnixville** Pottery, Pa., about 1880
In the Pennsylvania Museum.

M1, M2, etc., on bowls, covered jars, bonbon dishes and occasionally on plates.

N1, N2, etc., on covered cheese and sardine boxes.

O1, O2, etc., on cups and saucers.

These marks are given in detail to enable the investigator to recognize the ware produced here. All "majolica" so marked may confidently be attributed to this factory.

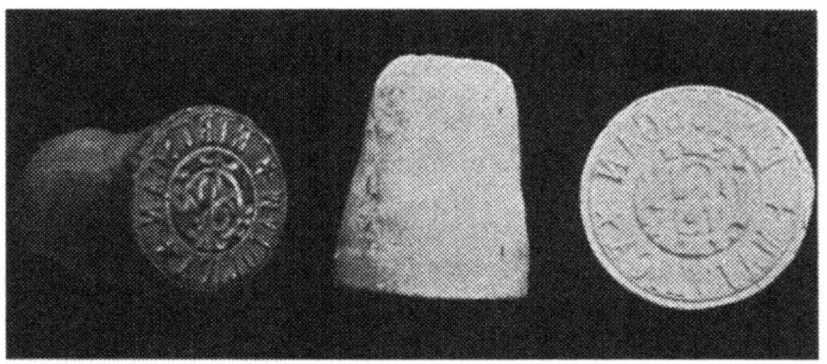

11. Baked Earthenware Stamps for Marking Majolica. Phœnixville Pottery, Pa.

On June 1, 1894, the works were leased by E. L. Buckwalter and H. I. Brownback, under the name of the Chester Pottery Company of Pennsylvania. The mark used by this firm in 1895 and 1896, on C. C. and semi-granite wares, was the Arms of Pennsylvania, printed in black under the glaze. In 1897 the Keystone mark was substituted, bearing the initials of the company. Later these letters were used alone. The name of the concern was changed to the Penn China Co. in 1899.

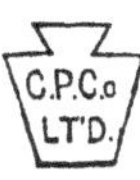


This pottery passed into new hands the first of January, 1902, the style being changed to the Tuxedo Pottery Co., the products being semi-granite, colored glaze ware and flow blue underglaze. No marks were used. Before the expiration of the year the works were again closed.

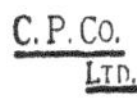

## THE PHILADELPHIA CITY POTTERY.

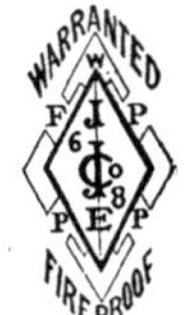


Messrs. J. E. Jeffords & Co. commenced potting in Philadelphia in 1868, Mr. Jeffords having learned the business with Morrison & Carr in New York. Their products are table and toilet white wares, jardinières and tea pots in colored glazes; Rockingham, yellow and blue glazed wares. They manufacture toby ale jugs and cow creamers in brown glaze, after the old shapes, and while not intended to deceive, these are such excellent reproductions of early patterns that examples frequently find their way into the shops of second-hand dealers and are sold as genuine antiques at high prices. Collectors would do well to familiarize themselves with these modern products, which have certain peculiarities of shape and modeling whereby they can be readily distinguished. The toby jugs have a deep, ball-shaped depression in the base, whereas older examples of the same form are more shallowly hollowed out or possess flat bottoms. Much of the ware made by this firm is unmarked.

At the Philadelphia exhibition of 1876 this firm made an exhibit of yellow, Rockingham, majolica and lava wares.

---

## GALLOWAY & GRAFF, PHILADELPHIA.

Galloway & Graff
Philadelphia.

Previous to the Centennial Exposition, Messrs. Galloway & Graff were manufacturing fine terra-cotta statuary and vases in Greek shapes for decorators. Their mark was the firm name impressed.

Galloway & Graff had an exhibit at the Centennial Exposition of statuary, vases, tazzas, pedestals, fountains, flower-pots and garden edging.

The factory, which was established in 1810, is now operated in West Philadelphia by Mr. William Galloway.

## THE MAYER POTTERY CO., LTD., BEAVER FALLS, PA.

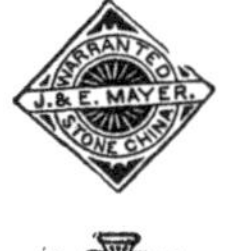


The Mayer Pottery Co. was organized in 1881. Their productions have been white granite table and toilet ware, underglaze decorations and colored glazes. At present their specialty is semi-vitreous china, plain and decorated.

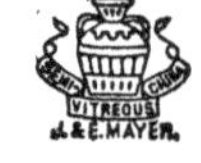


White granite ware was marked, between 1881 and 1891, with a square inclosing a circle, and the firm name, J. & E. Mayer.

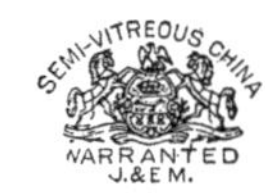


The vase and scroll mark was placed on semi-vitreous china and on overglaze decorated dinner and tea services.

The Arms of the State of Pennsylvania was used on semi-vitreous china.

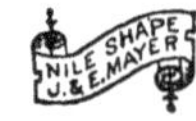


The "Nile" and "Amazon" shapes were for toilet use, the marks being scrolls bearing the names.

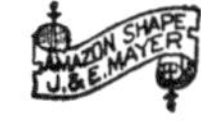


The following marks have been used on special patterns of underglaze printed table ware:

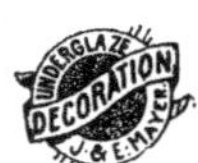

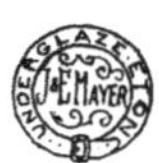


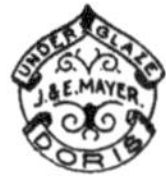


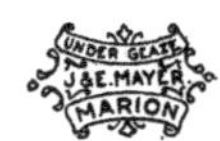


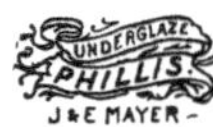


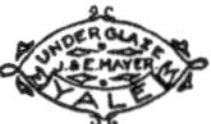


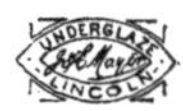


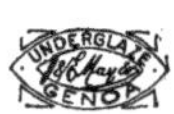


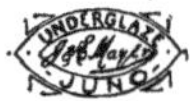


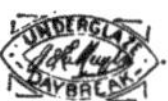


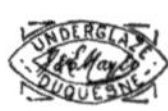


The majority of the above figured marks are transferred to the ware from engraved copperplates.

Additional marks of this company were used on the "Harvard," "Columbia" and "Duquesne" patterns, printed beneath the glaze in various colors,—black, green, gray, etc. Previous to the fire which destroyed much valuable property at this factory, in 1896, other marks were used on special services, such as the "Diana," "Potomac" and "Windsor" patterns.

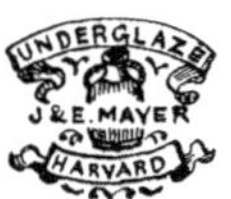


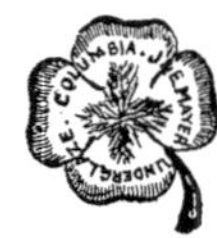


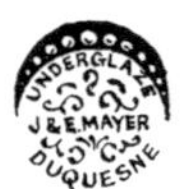


---

## STAR ENCAUSTIC TILE CO., PITTSBURGH, PA.

S.E.T.
CO.

This company was organized in 1882, succeeding to the business of the Pittsburgh Encaustic Tile Co., which began operations in 1876. The principal products have been unglazed encaustic tiles for flooring and pavements. The mark consists of the initials of the company, *impressed*.

---

## THE ROBERTSON ART TILE CO., MORRISVILLE, PA.

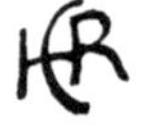

Hugh C. Robertson, of Dedham, Mass., modeled a number of embossed tile designs for the Robertson Art Tile Co., of Morrisville, Pa. His work was marked with his monogram.

---

## THE SHENANGO CHINA CO., NEWCASTLE, PA.

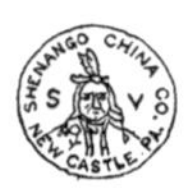


This company produces semi-vitreous china, plain and decorated. The mark is an Indian's head.

## MORAVIAN POTTERY AND TILE WORKS, DOYLESTOWN, PA.

Henry C. Mercer began experiments in the manufacture of art tiles several years ago at Doylestown, Pa. The common red clay of the vicinity is used, which is covered with a heavy enamel or colored glaze. The decorative motives, such as the conventionalized tulip, were suggested by the old iron stove plates and earthenware of the Pennsylvania Germans, which were produced in that section for more than 150 years. Lately Mr. Mercer has turned his attention to the reproduction of the old earthenware itself, with its quaint sgraffito designs and curious Pennsylvania-German inscriptions. He has named his establishment the Moravian Pottery and Tile Works.

Among recent styles attempted by Mr. Mercer are unglazed, smear glazed, modeled, sgraffito and slip-decorated tiles, many of the patterns being reproductions of mediæval designs found in England, Germany and other parts of Europe. He has also produced some large tile panels in which the decorative work is in modeled reliefs or composed of inlaid pieces of burned clay of different colors, in the style of bold mosaics. The enamel colors which he has succeeded in applying to the red brick clay body are of great variety, many of them being of rich, dull tones, exceedingly artistic and pleasing.

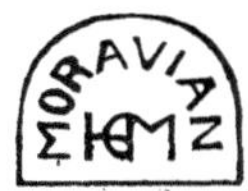

The mark is composed of the name of the pottery and the maker's monogram, enclosed in an arch. This is *impressed* in the ware. A variation of this mark is the word MORAVIAN stamped in the clay in large type.

**MORAVIAN**

---

## THE WICK CHINA CO., KITTANNING, PA.

The Wick China Co. manufactures ironstone china and decorated ware. The mark is a circle enclosing a monogram, used on "Aurora" china.

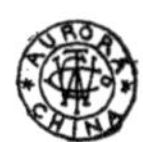

## THE FORD CHINA CO., FORD CITY, PA.

The Ford China Co. manufactures toilet and table ware, which is marked with the names of the patterns, "Victor," "Turin," "Leeds," "Bristol" and "Derby."

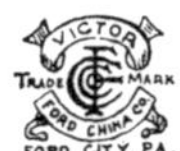

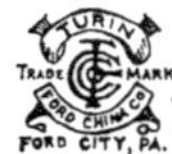

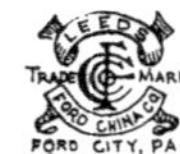

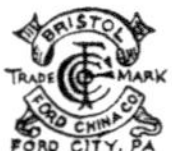

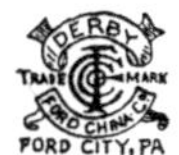


---

## THE NEWCASTLE POTTERY CO., NEWCASTLE, PA.

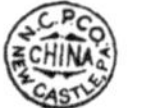


The Newcastle Pottery Co. has been recently organized. The only mark that has as yet been used is here shown.

---

## THE DERRY CHINA CO., DERRY STATION, PA.

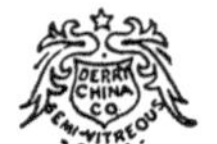


The Derry China Co. manufactures and decorates semi-vitreous china.

---

## THE PENNSYLVANIA MUSEUM AND SCHOOL OF INDUSTRIAL ART, PHILADELPHIA.

A School of Pottery was added to the course of this institution in the autumn of 1903, for the purpose of furnishing instruction in ceramic designing, modeling, decorating and the manufacture of art pottery. A suitable plant has been constructed with an up-to-date kiln and the necessary appliances for practical work in pottery-making, through all the stages, from the preparation of the clay to the final baking of the ware. Mr. Leon Volkmar, of the Menlo Park Pottery, has been placed at the head of this department.

During the first six months the Pottery School has made remarkable progress, and the exhibit of pottery from the new kiln is most gratifying. The decorations are modeled and carved in relief, and some of them show a marked ability and originality in this style of decorative work. The prevailing

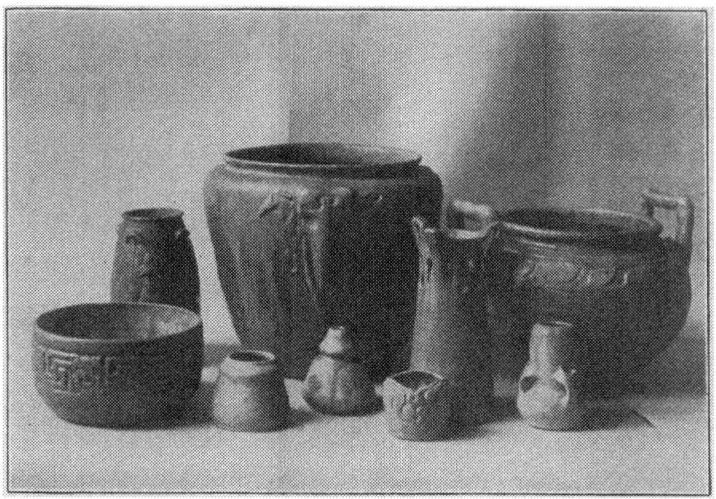

12. Group of Carved and Enameled Pottery.
Made by the Students of the School of Industrial Art of the Pennsylvania Museum.

color of the ware is green, but there are some beautiful shades of yellow enamels and a variety of blues. The greater portion of the ware possesses a matt surface, but some of the pieces are covered with a brilliant glaze. A striking piece is a large jardinière with modeled elephants' heads in low relief, and a large garden vase with five ear-like handles, on each of which is a modeled grotesque head in low relief, of extraordinary size and beautiful workmanship, possesses unusual merit. Great things may be expected from this department of the School, among which will be the development, in the direction of underglaze decoration, of a distinctive style of art ware, which in the near future cannot fail to bring the School prominently before the public.

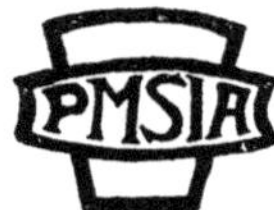


The mark which has been adopted for all ware produced here is a keystone, across which stretches an oval panel bearing the initials of the institution. In addition to this a date mark and record mark are used and the monogram or private mark of the decorator.

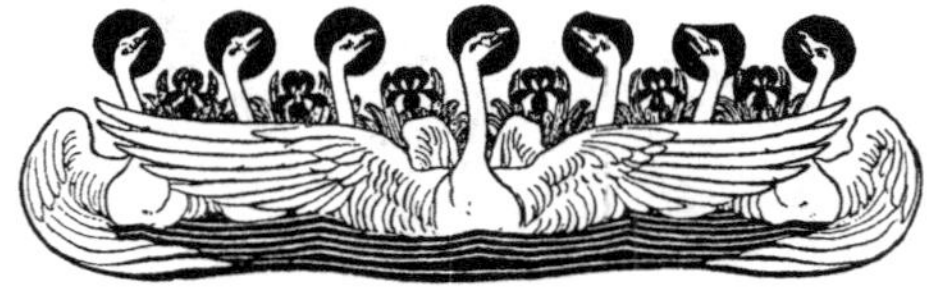

# NEW JERSEY POTTERIES

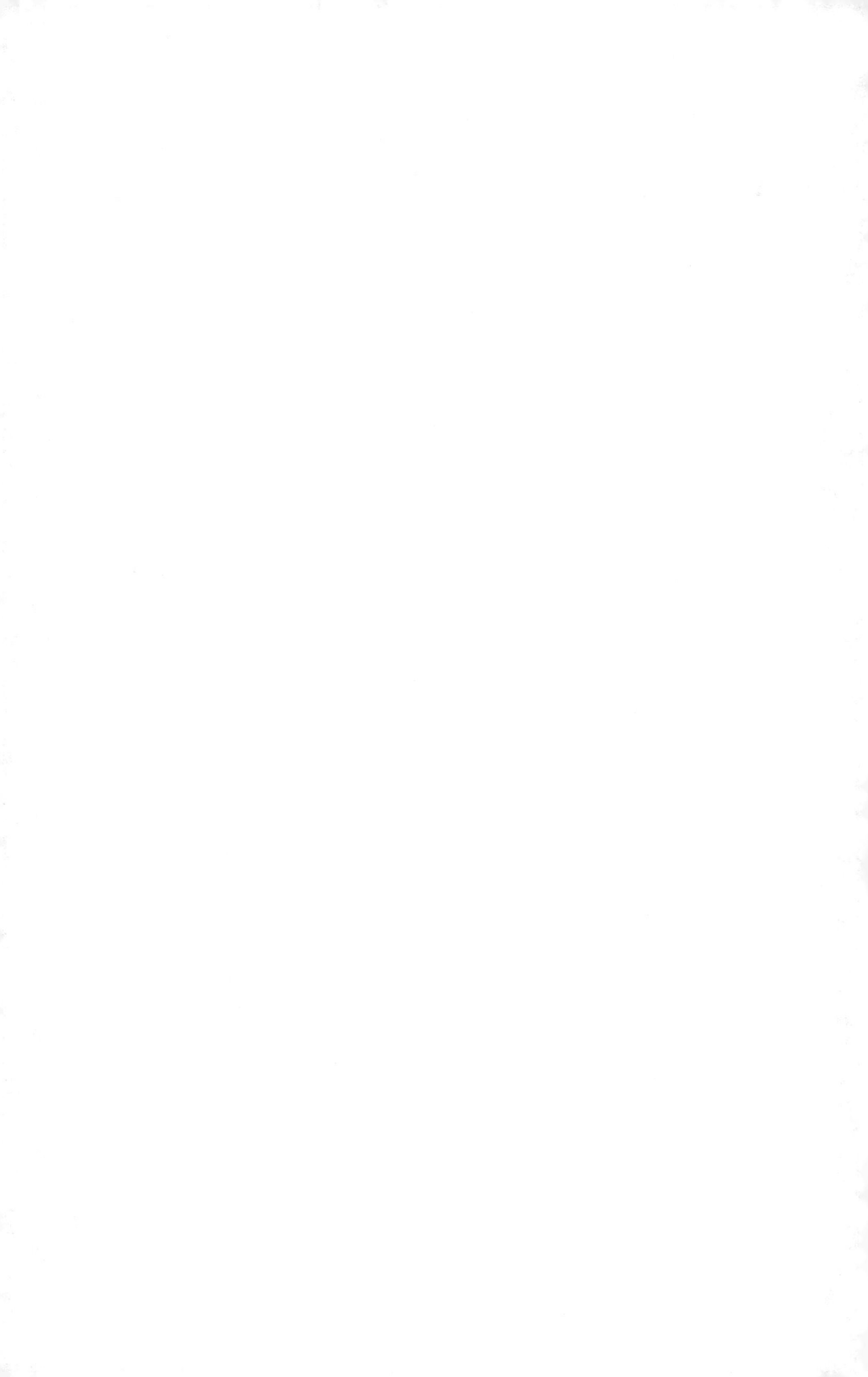

# NEW JERSEY POTTERIES.

## THE JERSEY CITY POTTERY, JERSEY CITY, N. J.

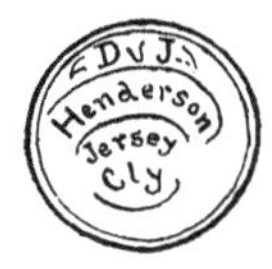


THE Jersey City Pottery Co. was operated by D. & J. Henderson about 1829, and the mark used by them was a circle enclosing their firm name and "Jersey City." This was *impressed* on brown glazed ware, such as toby jugs and hunting pitchers. Prof. John M. Clarke, of Albany, N. Y., owns a yellow ware pitcher, with relief decoration of oak leaves and acorns, so marked. An unmarked example may be seen in the Pennsylvania Museum (see illustration 13).

David Henderson organized the American Pottery Manufacturing Company in 1833. Several marks were in use at this time and during the next seven or eight years. About 1840 the English method of transfer printing was introduced for the first time in America. The flag mark, bearing the title of the company, was *printed* under the glaze in black. It is found on pitchers decorated with printed busts of General William Henry Harrison, the Log Cabin and American Eagle (see illustration 15).

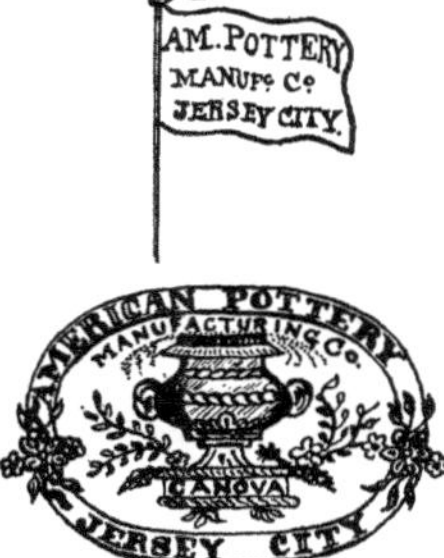


About the same time a large elliptical mark, upwards of two inches in width, was printed beneath the glaze, in light blue, and possibly in other colors. It is found on plates decorated with a printed pattern, known as the CANOVA design, which was copied from a transfer print issued by John Ridgway, of Hanley, England (see illustration 16).

AMERICAN POTT'Y CO
JERSEY CITY

The name of the corporation was changed to the American Pottery Co. about 1840. Several different marks of this period are known. One consists of the name arranged in straight lines and *impressed* by means of type. This mark was used on yellow ware for kitchen and table use in 1842.

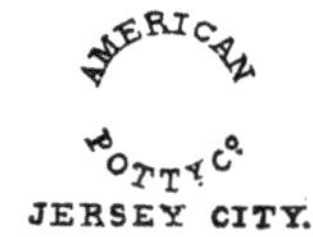


From 1840 to 1845 another impressed mark, consisting of the words "American Pottery Co.," arranged in a circle, and "Jersey City" in a straight line beneath, was in use. One of

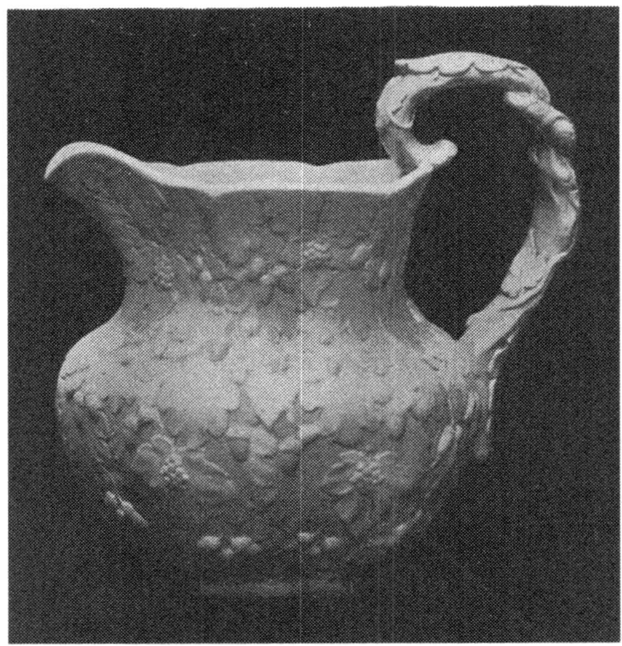

13. Yellow Ware Pitcher. Acorn Decoration in Relief.
By D. & J. Henderson, Jersey City Pottery, about 1830.
In the Pennsylvania Museum.

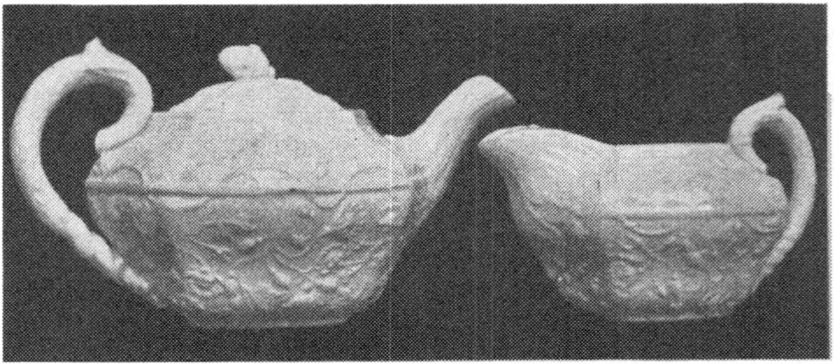

14. Teapot and Creamer. White Ware, Relief Decoration.
Jersey City Pottery, about 1840. In the Pennsylvania Museum.

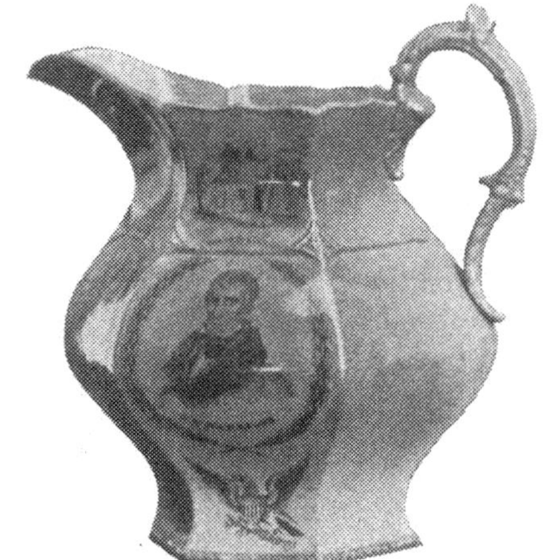

15. Harrison Cream ware Pitcher.
Printed Decoration.
Jersey City Pottery, 1840.

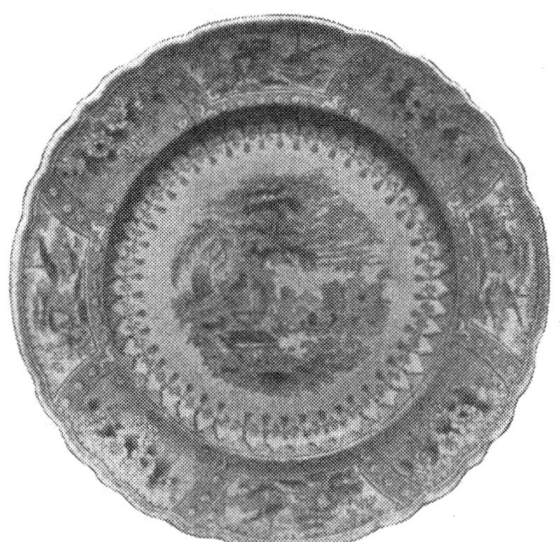

16. "Canova" Plate.
Printed Decoration.
Jersey City Pottery, about 1840.
In the Pennsylvania Museum.

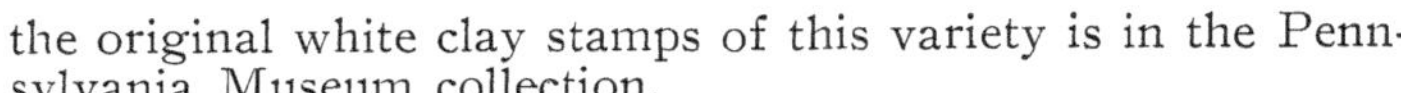
the original white clay stamps of this variety is in the Pennsylvania Museum collection.

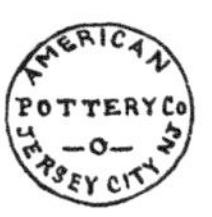


The same words, with the addition of the initials of the State (N. J.), were also enclosed in a circular stamp and impressed on Rockingham pitchers and jugs. Also found on cream-ware tea services, with relief ornamentation (see illustration 14).

Messrs. Rouse and Turner took the Jersey City Pottery soon after 1850. They made white ware, on which they placed the English mark, the lion and unicorn, with the initials of the firm, R. & T., beneath. This was probably the first American pottery to stamp its wares with a foreign mark. It was the beginning of a practice which afterwards became common among American manufacturers and has survived until the present time, for, until a few years ago, foreign wares were preferred to the domestic.

About 1880 the firm began to use a new mark on their ivory white ware for decorators. This mark consisted of the letters I. V. W. It was evidently prepared hurriedly, as the middle letter should have been a W, but, since the error had appeared on the ware, it was never corrected.

In the autumn of 1892 the old buildings, which had stood for nearly three-quarters of a century, were torn down, to make room for modern improvements.

---

## WILLIAM YOUNG & SONS, TRENTON, N. J.

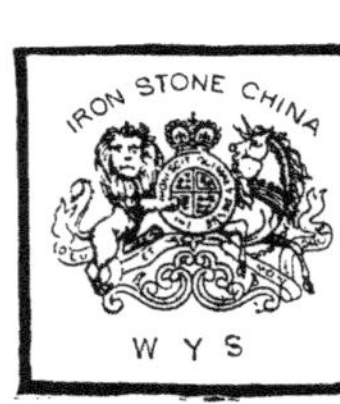


In 1853 William Young, in connection with his son, Wm. Young, Jr., commenced the manufacture of earthenware in Trenton, in a small pottery leased from Charles Hattersley, which had been built in the preceding year. For four years they made hardware porcelain, some china vases, pitchers of various kinds and a few dishes. In 1854 the pitcher, "Babes in the Wood," and a small china vase were issued.

In 1857 a new pottery was started under the name of the Excelsior Pottery Works, which was operated by William Young & Sons (William, Jr., Edward and John) until 1870, at which time William, Sr., withdrew, and for the following nine years the business was conducted by William Young's Sons.

The marks used were, in 1858, an eagle; from 1858 to 1879, the English Arms.

William Young, Sr. learned the art in the pottery of John Ridgway, of Hanley, England. He afterwards went into business for himself and subsequently came to this country. At the Centennial Exposition the firm was awarded a bronze medal for superior goods. Their exhibit consisted of crockery, porcelain and hardware trimmings.

---

## THE WILLETS MANUFACTURING CO., TRENTON, N. J.

In 1879 the Willets Mfg. Co. came into possession of the works formerly operated by Wm. Young & Sons, and still retain them. The plant has since been extended from time to time, until it is now one of the largest in this country.

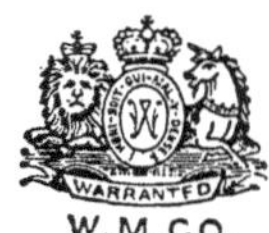


The marks used by the Willets Mfg. Co. are as follows: On stone china, the Arms of Great Britain. In 1884 a monogram was adopted, composed of the firm name, which was either impressed on white granite ware or applied in color. On their semi-porcelain they have used an octagonal mark, and on table and toilet wares printed pattern marks have been used, such as "Arno," "Duchess," "Forget-me-not," "Adelaide," "Saratoga," etc. On decorated Belleek china they have used two marks, formed of a serpent twisted to represent the letter W, one having the word Belleek above. These are printed on the glaze in red, brown or black.

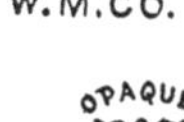


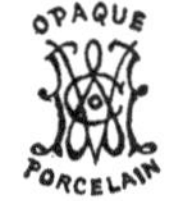


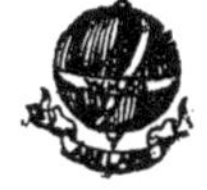

Other wares manufactured at different times by this company were thin and hotel white granite, majolica, porcelain door knobs and hardware trimmings and electric goods.

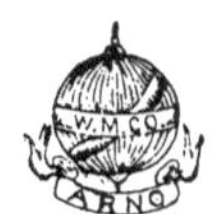

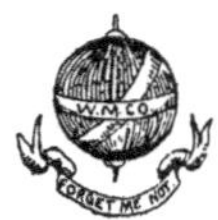


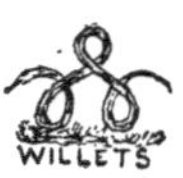


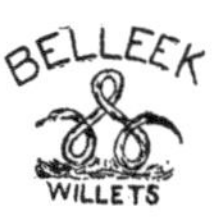

## THE CITY POTTERY, TRENTON, N. J.

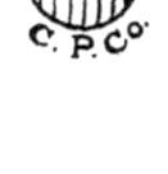

Messrs. Rhodes & Yates, of the City Pottery, Trenton, were the first in that place to manufacture white granite and cream-colored wares exclusively. They began in 1859, on the site of the old Hattersley Pottery, and in 1860 received a medal from the New Jersey State Agricultural Society for the best white granite ware. In 1865 the style became Yates & Titus. They were succeeded in 1871 by Messrs. Yates, Bennett & Allan. In the latter year the English mark was used in connection with their initials, Y. B. A. In 1875, when the City Pottery Co. was incorporated, the same mark, with the letters C. P. Co., was employed. In 1876 a new mark was introduced, a shield, bearing the same letters. In that year the company exhibited table and toilet wares at the Centennial Exposition. The pottery continued in operation for several years after that date.

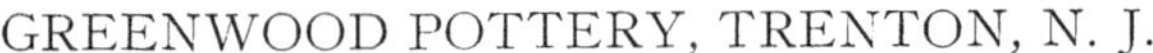

## GREENWOOD POTTERY, TRENTON, N. J.

Messrs. Stephens, Tams & Co. established a pottery in Trenton in 1861. In 1868 they organized the Greenwood Pottery Co. From the latter date until 1875 the Arms of the State of New Jersey were used as a mark for ironstone china or white granite. In the last-named year they added the legend which appears on the subjoined mark. The patent was on a scalloped dish which was produced at that time.

G. P.
Co.

The initials of the company were stamped in the body of the first table porcelain made at this factory about the same period.

GREENWOOD CHINA
TRENTON, N.J.

In 1886 the name "Greenwood China" was *impressed* in the body of table and toilet wares.

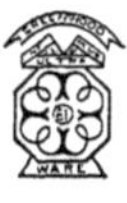

From 1883 to 1886 the mark used on art wares was suggested by the Royal Worcester mark. The figures in the centre (61) have reference to the date of the establishment of the factory. This mark was printed in purple on the ware, which had an ivory finish and raised gold decorations.

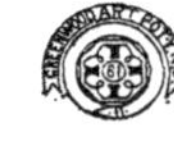

In 1886 the mark used on porcelain art ware was a modification of the above. It was printed in purple beneath the glaze.

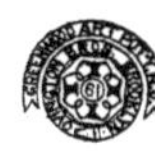

This same device was also used on special orders of art goods for Messrs. Ovington Bros., of Brooklyn, N. Y., with the addition of their firm name.

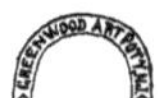

The upper portion of this mark was also used alone, to some extent, on similar wares, of the Royal Worcester style.

---

## THE EAST TRENTON POTTERY CO., TRENTON, N. J.

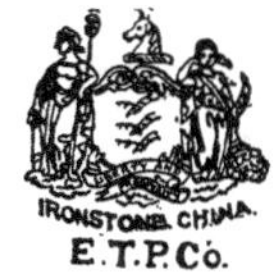


In 1888 this company was producing china or white granite ware bearing printed portraits of the Presidential candidates. The mark then used consisted of the Arms of the State of New Jersey.

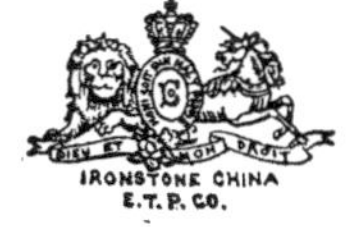


Later, the mark, "Opaque China, E. T. P. Co.," was *impressed* in the paste.

On white granite ware the British lion and unicorn mark was also employed.

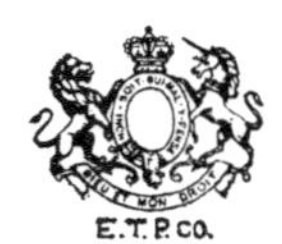


A variation of this device, with the lion and unicorn *standing*, was also in use. These appeared on toilet and table services, printed in black beneath the glaze.

---

## MILLINGTON, ASTBURY & POULSON, TRENTON, N. J.

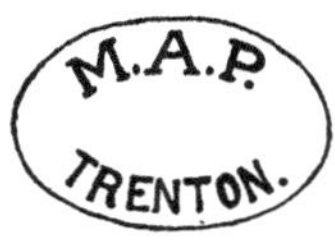


Richard Millington and John Astbury, under the style of Millington & Astbury, established a pottery in Carroll Street in 1853. In 1859 the firm name became Millington, Astbury & Poulson. They were making white ware goods in 1861. A large pitcher, with relief designs, illustrating the shooting of Col. E. E. Ellsworth, at Alexandria, Va., at the breaking out of the Civil War, bears their *impressed* mark, an ellipse with the initials of the firm name. This pitcher occurs both

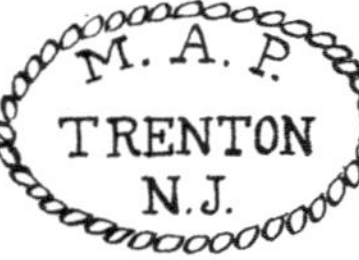


in white and in brilliant coloring. It was modeled by Josiah Jones, a noted modeler of the period. A modification of the same mark was sometimes stamped in their white granite ware. The colored examples were painted by Edward Lycett, a decorator of New York City.

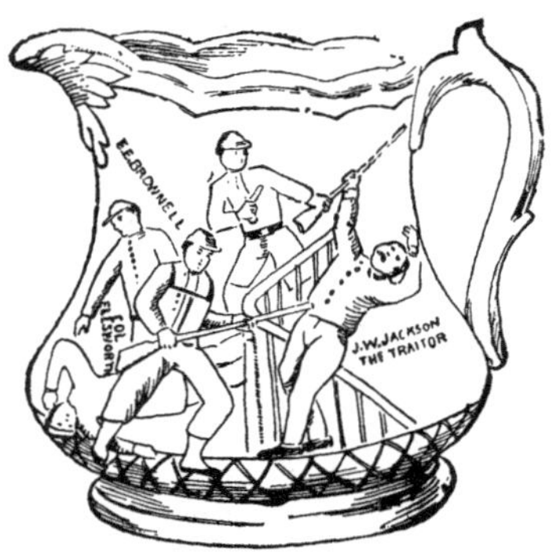


17. Ellsworth Pitcher.
Designs in Relief and Colored.
Millington, Astbury & Poulson,
Trenton, N. J., 1861.

The credit of modeling this jug has been claimed for others, but Mr. Thomas Maddock, who afterwards entered the firm, has settled the question by informing the writer that it was unquestionably the work of Mr. Jones.

---

## THOMAS MADDOCK & SONS, TRENTON, N. J.

About the year 1861, Mr. Poulson, of the above-mentioned firm, died, and a Mr. Coughley took his interest in the concern. About 1869 Mr. Coughley died, and Mr. Thomas Maddock bought up his interest and also that of Mr. Millington, who then started the Eagle Pottery in the same city. In

1876 the firm was Astbury & Maddock. At the Centennial they exhibited sanitary earthenware and crockery for general use. Later Mr. Maddock became sole owner of the plant, and took his sons into partnership. The marks used by Thomas Maddock & Sons are: A circular ribbon containing the initials of the firm name and the date 1859, surmounted by a crown, which was used on dinner ware, and an anchor for sanitary earthenware.

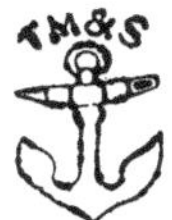


---

## THE MADDOCK POTTERY CO., TRENTON, N. J.

This company dates from the year 1893, operating what is known as the Lamberton Works. Thomas Maddock & Sons, Moses Collear, C. A. May and Thomas P. Donoher are the stockholders. They manufacture fine grades of semi-porcelain in table and toilet wares.

The factory mark bears the name of the works. The mark for decorated china is a crown, while that for undecorated ware is the word CHINA, with the initials M (Maddock) and L (Lamberton) above and below.

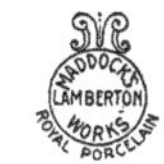


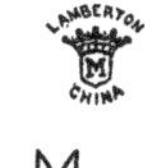


M<br>CHINA<br>L

---

## JOHN MADDOCK & SONS, TRENTON, N. J.

John Maddock & Sons, of the Coalport Works, commenced the manufacture of steamship, car builders' and plumbers' earthenware and sanitary specialties of every description in 1894. Mr. John Maddock is a son of Mr. Thomas Maddock, of Thomas Maddock & Sons, having associated with him his own sons. Their marks are, for "Coalport" china, a four-leaf clover, which occurs in two varieties.

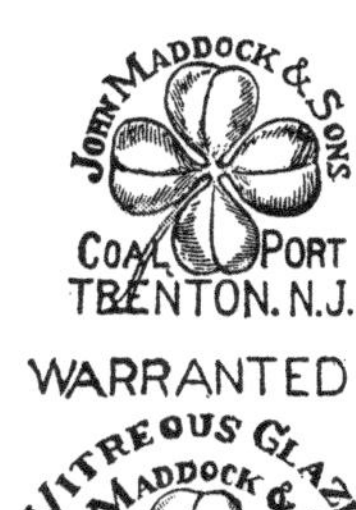


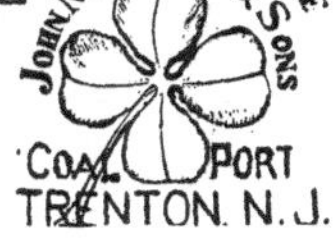

## THE GLASGOW POTTERY, TRENTON, N. J.

John Moses founded the Glasgow Pottery in 1863. The principal products have been white granite and cream-colored wares, thin hotel and steamboat china. Just previous to the Centennial large quantities of souvenir cups and saucers were made at this factory for the Centennial Tea Parties which were held in various parts of the country. The John Hancock cups and saucers were exceedingly popular, and many of them are preserved in collections to-day.

The Glasgow Pottery Co. exhibited at the Centennial stone china, decorated ware and majolica.

GLASGOW POTTERY
— CO. —
TRENTON
N.J.

One of the earliest marks of the Glasgow Pottery was the name printed in black on white granite ware. A modification of this has recently been in use by the John Moses & Sons Co., by which title the present firm is known.

IRONSTONE CHINA
J.M. & Co.

Another mark used in 1876 was the American eagle and shield, on white granite.

A similar mark was used on semi-porcelain in 1878.

In 1880 a wreath enclosing the date was the mark for the same ware.

In 1882 white granite was marked "Glasgow China," in a circle.

In 1884 the monogram of John Moses, surrounded by the name of the ware, was printed on white granite in black.

On the same grade of ware, in 1893, a diamond-shaped mark was printed.

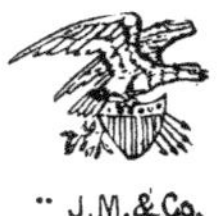

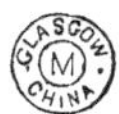


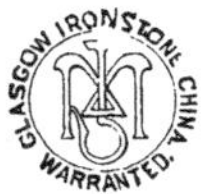


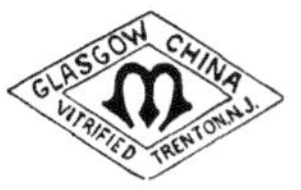


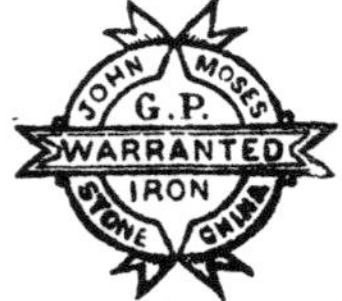


An additional mark used by John Moses, on white granite, is here shown.

A circular mark was used on opaque porcelain.

The Arms of Great Britain was used by John Moses & Co. on ironstone china, or white granite.

The marks of John Moses & Sons Co. are several varieties of the British Coat of Arms for white granite, used from about 1895 to the present time.

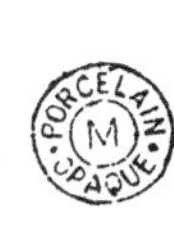

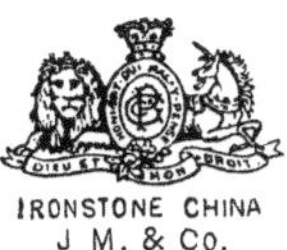

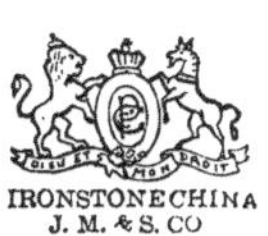

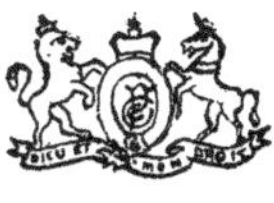
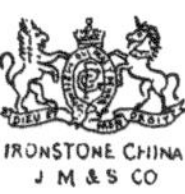


Mark for vitrified china.

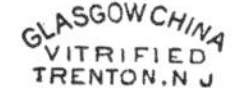


The various marks used by this firm on toilet and table services to indicate the patterns are as follows:

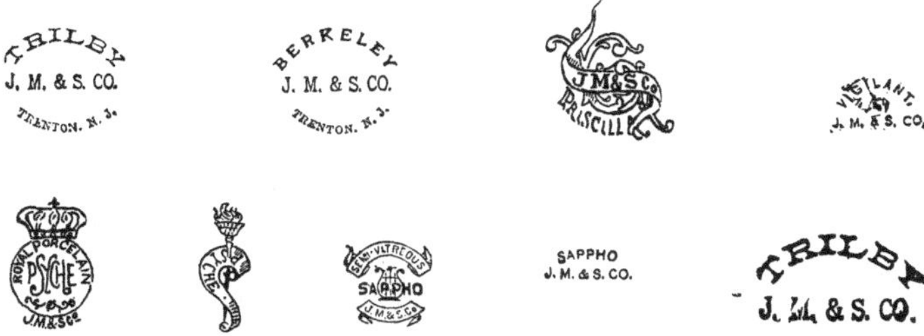


In 1899 the Glasgow Pottery made, by order of the United States Government, crockery for the use of the National Home for Disabled Volunteer Soldiers, on which was required to be printed the seal of the institution. The date on the seal, March 3, 1865, is the date of the approval of the act of Congress establishing the Home.

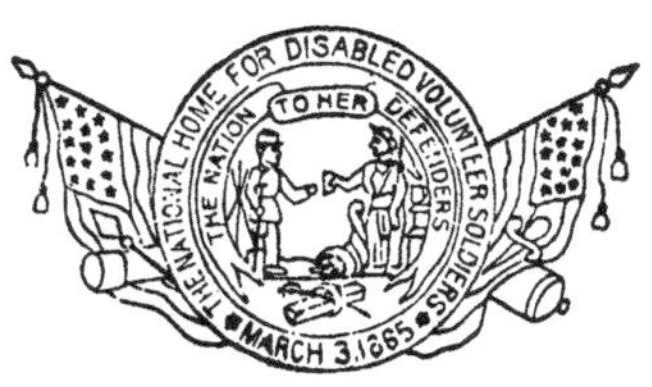


The same firm manufactured ware for the Quartermaster's Department, which was stamped Q. M. D.

**Q.M.D.**

They were also the contracting potters for furnishing crockery for the United States Marine Corps, on which was stamped the letters U. S. M. C.

**U.S.M.C.**

Special marks were also used for other branches of the Government service, such as the Navy and the Medical Board.

Other marks were placed on special orders of dealers in various parts of the country, of which the following are a few:

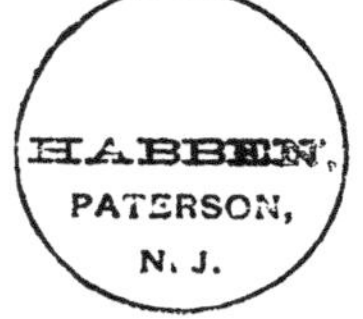


ALBERT PICK & CO.
CHICAGO.

G. H. Kittredge.

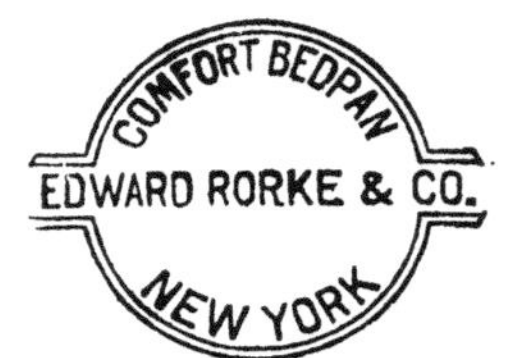


## OTT & BREWER, TRENTON, N. J.

The Etruria Pottery dates back to 1863, in which year it was built by Messrs. Bloor, Ott & Booth. John Hart Brewer entered the firm in 1865, and the style soon after become Ott & Brewer.

The marks for white granite were variations of the British Coat of Arms.

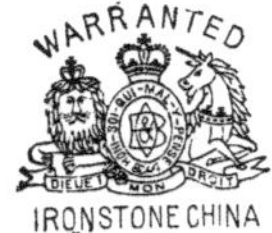


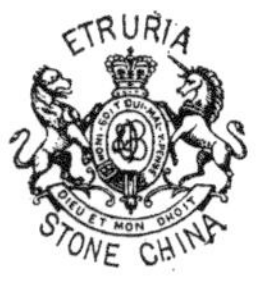


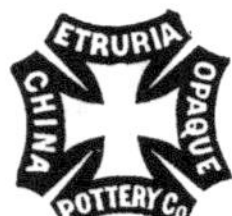


Opaque china table wares were marked with a Maltese Cross surrounded by a ribbon, and occasionally with a circular rising sun device containing the firm name.

A common mark on table ware consisted of the initials of the firm name over the word "China."

The monogram of the firm in a circle was placed on a fine grade of china.

Semi-porcelain ware was marked with a globe, and occasionally with a "Royal Crown."

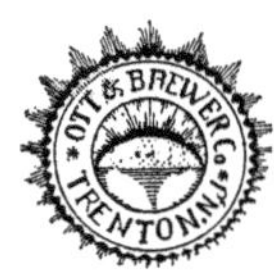


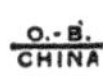


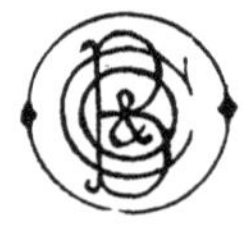

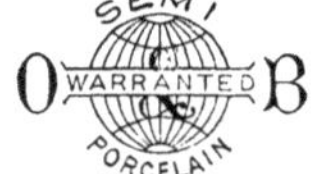


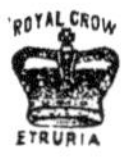


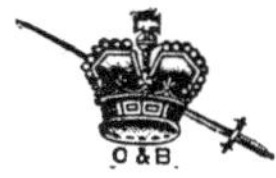


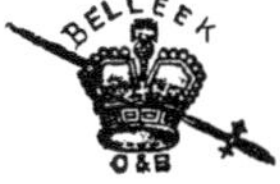


In 1876 this firm exhibited at the Centennial Exposition, attracting much attention through their Parian portrait busts and figure vases, which had been modeled by Prof. Isaac Broome. This firm was the first to commence the manufacture of Belleek ware in this country. In 1882 some workmen from the Irish Belleek works were brought over for this purpose, and the manufacture of thin egg-shell china with lustre glazes was established in Trenton.

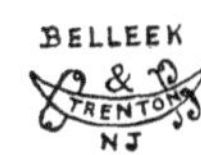

Several marks were used on Etruria Belleek, among which are two varieties of the crown and sword, and two of the crescent, designs, which were printed over the glaze in red or brown. Occasionally the same ware was marked "Manufactured by Ott & Brewer, Trenton, N. J., U. S. A.," and again with the firm name in a circle. The initials of the firm were also used on fine Belleek ware about 1885.

MANUFACTURED BY
OTT & BREWER
TRENTON, N.J. U.S.A.

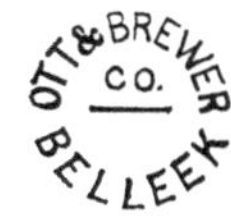


The junior member of the firm was particularly active in experimenting in new bodies and developing the artistic features of the manufacture. Among the many different styles attempted were modeled vases in Belleek body with relief cactus decoration; pate-sur-pate work in which the designs were painted in white slip on colored grounds; cameo effects, produced by applying relief ornaments and portrait heads of one color to tinted bodies in different tones.

A few years ago this firm was succeeded by the Cook Pottery Co.

O. & B.

## THE COOK POTTERY COMPANY, TRENTON, N. J.

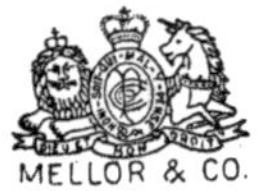


This company was organized in the early part of 1894, succeeding to the business of Messrs. Ott & Brewer. The officers are: Charles Howell Cook, President; F. G. Mellor, Vice-President and Treasurer, and James J. Mulheron, Secretary.

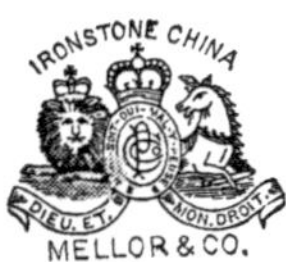


Their mark for C. C. ware was the British Lion and Unicorn, with shield bearing the monogram of the Cook Pottery Co. with the name Mellor & Co. below. This mark was adopted for the purpose of avoiding any confusion between the products of this factory and the old Crescent Pottery, whose goods were then stamped "Cook & Hancock."

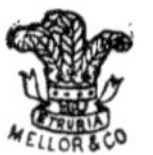


A similar mark was used on white granite ware.

On porcelain dinner ware two marks were used, one composed of three feathers, the other a circle enclosing the combined names of Etruria and Mellor & Co.

A four-leaf clover distinguished their *"Juno"* shape in semi-vitreous china.

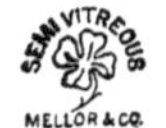


On Belleek ware the three feather mark was also used to some extent.

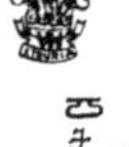

The Delft ware of the Cook Pottery Co. is the best imitation of the old Dutch faience which has been produced in this country. While the glaze is not stanniferous, it is an excellent simulation of the opaque enamel of Holland, and the tone of the blue color used in the decorations is a close approach to the genuine Delft. The mark is an adaptation of an old Holland mark.

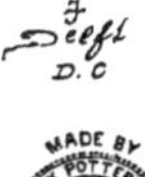

A special jug, made in commemoration of Admiral Dewey's victory at Manila, bears a circular mark with the date of patent, 1899.

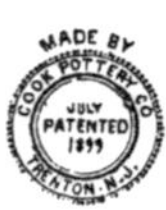


---

## ISAAC BROOME.

Prof. Isaac Broome, modeler for Ott & Brewer, produced on his own account some original ware in vitrified porcelain body in 1880. The body, the underglaze coloring and the glaze were thoroughly incorporated together, producing a

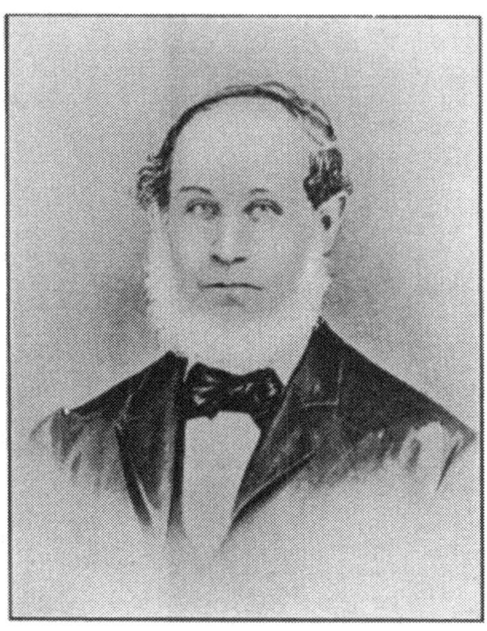

18. Portrait of Charles Coxon,
Modeler and Potter.
Born, 1805. Died, 1868.

soft, rich, mottled effect, different from any other ware produced in America. Only about 100 pieces, mostly small vases, were made, and these were soon absorbed in private collections, and highly valued. They were marked with an arbitrary device, a modification of the sign of the planet Jupiter, similar to the mark on old Plymouth (England) porcelain. It was scratched in the body below the glaze.

BROOME

Prof. Broome formerly modeled for the Providential Tile Works and the Trent Tile Co., of Trenton, N. J., and later for the Beaver Falls Art Tile Co. Many of his relief tile designs were marked on the face with his monogram, or with his name *impressed*.

## COXON & CO., TRENTON, N. J.

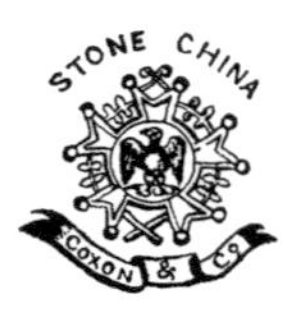


The firm of Coxon & Co. was established in 1863, in Trenton, by Charles Coxon and J. F. Thompson. Mr. Coxon had been a modeler at the pottery of Edwin and William Bennett, Baltimore, for about twelve years. Their products were cream-colored ware and white granite. The mark was a badge with the American eagle in the centre and the name of the firm in a ribbon beneath, printed in black under the glaze. Mr. Coxon died in 1868, and the pottery was operated for a time by his widow and four sons, John, Charles, Frank and Jonathan, all practical potters. In 1876 they made pieces decorated with printed views of some of the Centennial buildings. About 1884 the works were sold to Alpaugh & Magowan, who gave them the name of the Empire Pottery.

## THE TRENTON POTTERY CO.

T. P. Co.
CHINA

This company was incorporated in New Jersey in 1865. One of the marks used, on white granite, consisted of the initials of the company printed in black. In 1870 the style was changed to Taylor, Goodwin & Co.

## THE MERCER POTTERY CO., TRENTON, N. J.

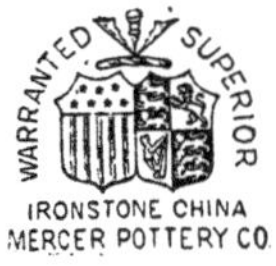


The Mercer Pottery Co. was organized in 1868. James Moses, the head of the company, claims to have been the first to make semi-porcelain ware in this country. The double shield mark, formerly used by this company, was the same as that employed by the firms of Carr & Clark and Burgess & Campbell (which see). It was also used at the New York City Pottery by Mr. Carr, as will be seen. When the International Pottery Co. was organized in 1879 by Messrs. Carr and Clark, assisted by John and James Moses, the double shield was adopted as being an appropriate design for the name of the company, Mr. Clark being an English potter and James Moses an American. The same shapes were being made at the Mercer and International Potteries and the goods were interchangeable. Hence the same mark was used by each, the only difference being in the name printed beneath. In September of the same year Messrs. Burgess & Campbell bought the interest of Carr & Clark and substituted their names beneath the trade-mark.

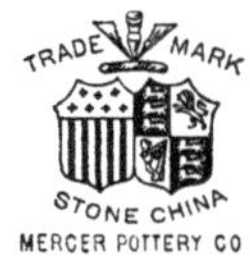


Other marks are a globe *impressed* on white granite ware.

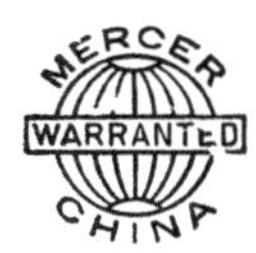


The name of the pottery, *impressed.*

MERCER POTTERY
TRENTON, N. J.

The initials of the pottery on ironstone china or white granite.

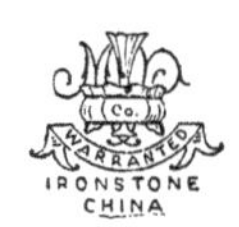


A shield on semi-vitreous china, with printed decorations.

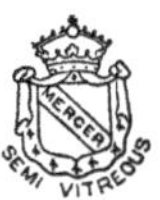


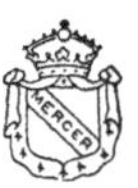


The monogram of the Company.

The following occur on various patterns of table and toilet services:

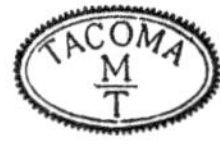

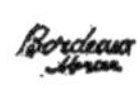

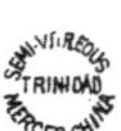

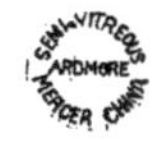

## THE NEW JERSEY POTTERY CO., TRENTON, N. J.

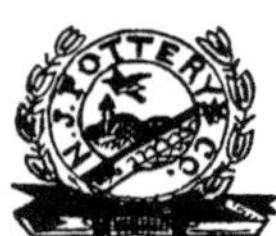


The New Jersey Pottery Co. was organized in 1869, at Trenton, and in 1883 the name was changed to the Union Pottery Co. The products were cream-colored and white granite wares. During the Presidential campaign of 1880 this company issued a series of plates with overglaze printed portraits of the candidates. The mark was printed in black beneath the glaze.

---

## INTERNATIONAL POTTERY CO., TRENTON, N. J.

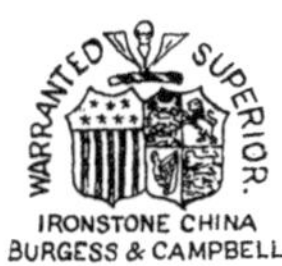


Henry Speeler established the International Pottery in 1860, and in 1868 admitted to partnership his two sons, under the name of Henry Speeler & Sons.

Edward Clark and James Carr purchased the Speeler* works, and in 1879 organized the Lincoln Pottery Co. A mark was adopted, with the name of the firm, Carr & Clark, beneath. A few months later the style was changed, and the same mark was continued after the reorganization by the International Pottery Co. The names of Burgess & Campbell, their successors, were substituted (see also James Carr, and the Mercer Pottery Co.).

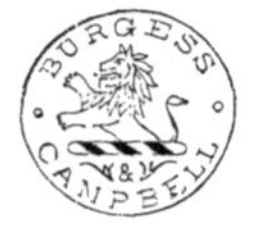


On certain patterns of underglaze ware a circular stamp was *impressed* in semi-porcelain.

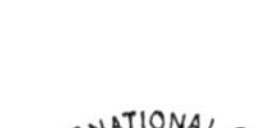


Another mark ("International China") was used on the same grade of ware.

On semi-porcelain table ware with blue decorations beneath the glaze, the "Royal Blue" marks were printed in the same color.

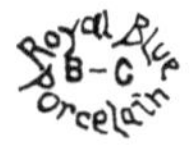


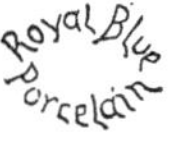


---

* The Speeler Pottery Co. exhibited yellow and Rockingham ware at the Philadelphia Exposition in 1876.

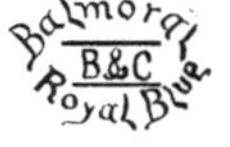


A similar mark was used on toilet and dinner ware of the "Balmoral" pattern.

Pattern marks were used on toilet and table wares, such as "Albany," "Japonica," "Lotus" and "Diamond."

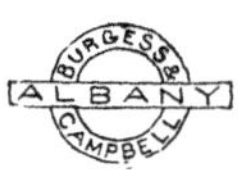


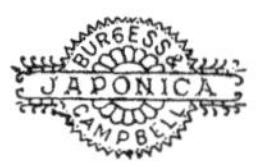


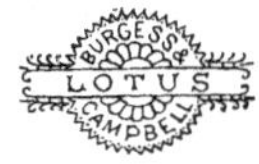


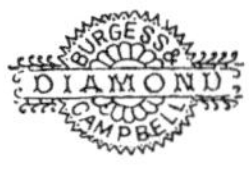


After the withdrawal of Mr. Campbell, the style became Burgess & Co. The mark used on "Royal China" in 1903 is a crown in a circle.

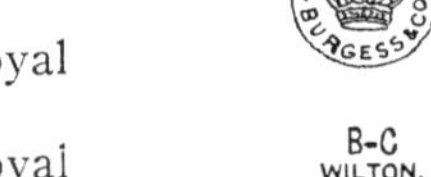


On "Wilton" china, of the same pattern as the "Royal Blue," decorated in "still blue" and gray underglaze.

Two additional marks were sometimes placed on "Royal Blue" ware.

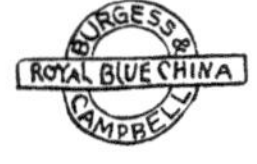


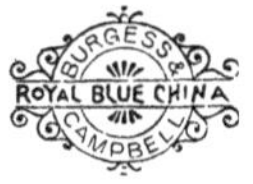


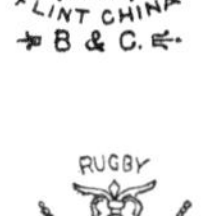


On the "Rugby" pattern, made in "Flint China," a grade of ware between white granite and porcelain, two marks were printed in brown.

Late marks of the International Pottery Co. used on semi-vitreous porcelain represent a Maltese cross.

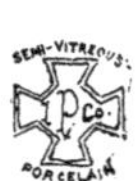


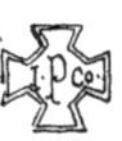


## THE AMERICAN CROCKERY CO., TRENTON, N. J.

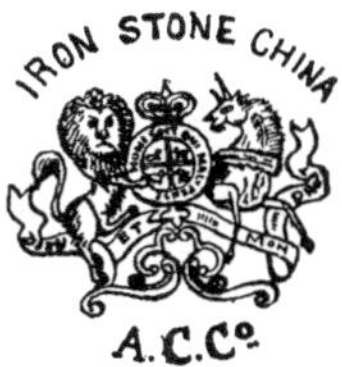


In 1876 the American Crockery Co. was manufacturing bisque and white granite wares, in which year an exhibit was made at the Centennial Exposition. The mark used on white granite was the English Lion and Unicorn, with the initials

AMERICAN CHINA
A.C.CO.

of the company beneath. This mark, printed in black, occurs on a small milk jug, decorated with a printed view of old Independence Hall, Philadelphia, now in the Pennsylvania Museum.

On a water jug, with transfer prints of Horticultural Hall and the Agricultural Building of the Centennial produced at the same period, is found the eagle and monogram mark, here given, which is printed in black beneath the glaze.

About 1890 the mark used by this company on white granite ware was printed in black.

---

## BURROUGHS & MOUNTFORD CO., TRENTON, N. J.

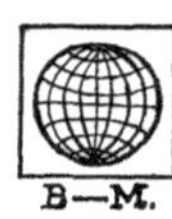


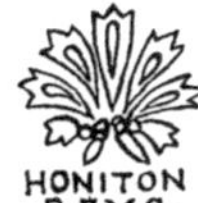

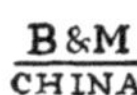


B–M.

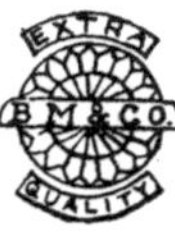


The Burroughs & Mountford Co. began business in Trenton in 1879, in the Eagle Pottery, erected in 1876 by Richard Millington. They produced a large line of table and toilet wares and a number of characteristic styles of art wares, in bold ornamentation and harmonious coloring. Some of their larger vases, painted by a Japanese artist in their employ, were among the finest pieces of the kind ever produced in this country. This firm discontinued business several years ago.

The globe mark was used on decorated wares, in "cretonne" patterns.

The "Honiton" mark appeared on a tea service with printed decorations.

The Crown mark and the initials of the firm were used on various grades of white granite and C. C. wares with printed decorations.

The "Extra Quality" mark was impressed in white granite table ware. It occurs on a plate bearing the decorative mark of the Harker Pottery Co., of East Liverpool, Ohio.

## THE PROSPECT HILL POTTERY, TRENTON, N. J.

In 1880 Messrs. Dale & Davis established the Prospect Hill Pottery, and continued to manufacture decorated semi-porcelain and white granite dinner and toilet wares until about 1894. Their earliest mark for white granite was the Arms of Great Britain. Later they used the initials of the firm name.

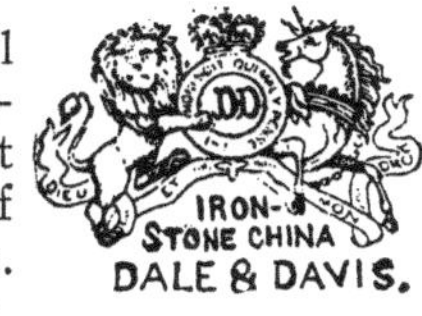


D—D

Previous to this partnership, from about 1875 to 1880, Isaac Davis was in business alone, and in 1876 made an exhibit of white granite ware at the Centennial Exposition. The lion and unicorn mark was used on print-decorated ware with views of historic American buildings. A bread plate in the Pennsylvania Museum, with view of Horticultural Hall, one of the Centennial buildings, bears this mark.

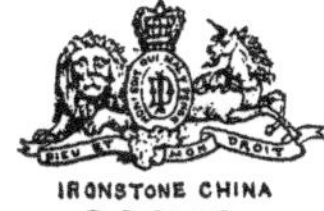


A similar mark was used on a patent in 1879.

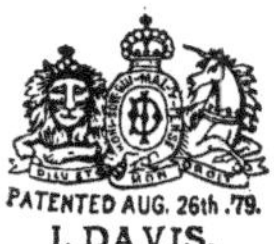


The mark for opaque porcelain was a draped shield bearing the figure of an eagle.

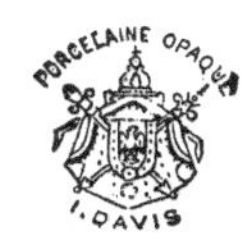


---

## THE ANCHOR POTTERY, TRENTON, N. J.

This pottery was established by James E. Norris, about 1894. The earlier marks were a modification of the British Arms and an anchor enclosed in a circle. Since 1898 the three following marks have been in use, the last two bearing the names of patterns or shapes.

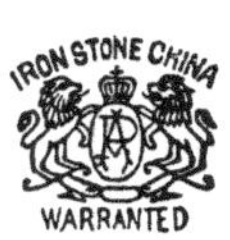


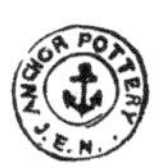


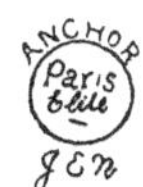


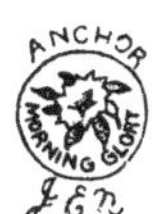

The later marks of this pottery, used on semi-porcelain ware, are shown below.

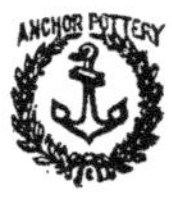


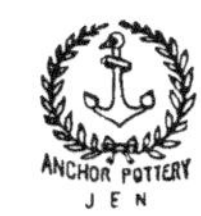


Berlin
ANCHOR POTTERY
J. E. N.

## THE DELAWARE POTTERY, TRENTON, N. J.

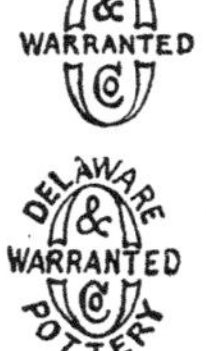


Messrs. Oliphant & Co. operated The Delaware Pottery between 1884 and 1895. The two marks here figured were *printed* in black, or *impressed* on cups, druggists' mortars, etc. A limited amount of Belleek porcelain was also made at one time by this firm (see also The Trenton Potteries Co.).

## THE CRESCENT POTTERY, TRENTON, N. J.

The Crescent Pottery Co. was organized in 1881 by Charles H. Cook and W. S. Hancock, for the manufacture of sanitary earthenware, white granite and C. C. wares.

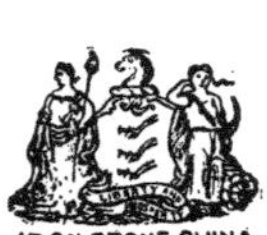


In 1885, their marks were the Coat of Arms of the State of New Jersey, and a lion's head in a circular garter, on white granite dinner ware.

About 1890, the lion mark, printed in black on white granite, or "Paris White" ware, was in use.

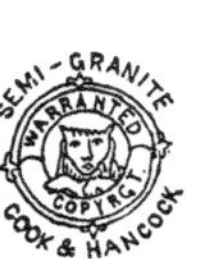


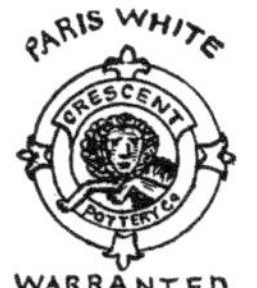


In 1890, the "Dainty" pattern mark was used.
In 1896, the "Melloria" pattern was issued.

DAINTY
COOK & HANCOCK.

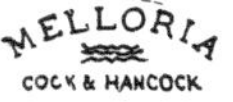

From 1896 to 1898, the "Melloria" and "Dainty" marks were placed on semi-granite dinner ware.

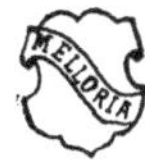


DAINTY

In the latter year the "Dainty" and "Severn" marks were used.

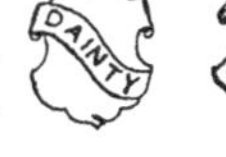

From 1899 to 1902 the globe, supported by a lion and unicorn, formed one of the factory marks for semi-granite dinner ware.

The "Utopia" mark was placed on underglaze decorated dinner ware from 1900 to 1902.

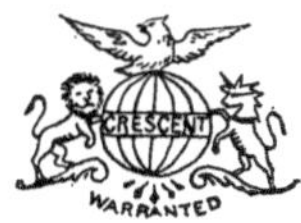


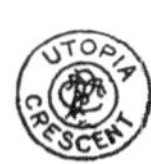


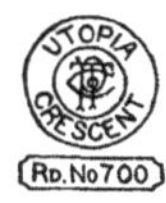


The same mark was used in 1901 on the "Alpha" pattern, in underglaze dinner and tea services (see also The Trenton Potteries Co.).

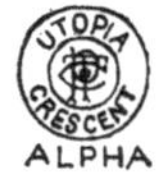


ALPHA

---

## EMPIRE POTTERY, TRENTON, N. J.

This pottery was established by Messrs. Coxon & Thompson in 1863. About 1884 it passed into the hands of Messrs. Alpaugh & Magowan, whose products were thin porcelain, dinner, tea and toilet wares, and decorated wares, principally in white granite body. They also made sanitary and plumbers' earthenware. One of the earliest marks used by the latter firm was the British Coat of Arms, which was placed on all their general ware.

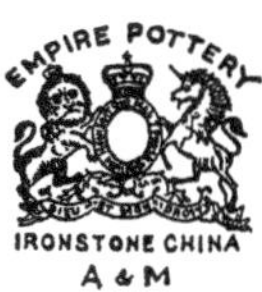


In Wood & Barlow's time, the "Imperial China" mark was in use.

About 1892 a wreath enclosing the monogram T. P. Co. was used (see also The Trenton Potteries Co.).

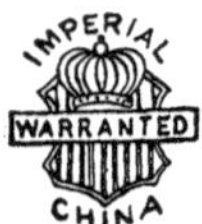


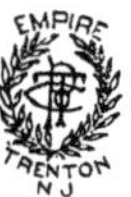


---

## THE ENTERPRISE POTTERY CO., TRENTON, N. J.

Enterprise
Pottery Co

The Enterprise Pottery was started previous to 1880, for the manufacture of sanitary ware. The mark in use from the beginning until 1892 was the name of the company (see also The Trenton Potteries Co.). Gen. Oliphant, who with three of his sons afterwards operated the Delaware Pottery, was connected with the Enterprise Pottery previous to 1884.

---

## THE TRENTON POTTERIES CO., TRENTON, N. J.

In 1892, The Trenton Potteries Co. was organized by the consolidation of five sanitary ware establishments,—The Crescent, The Delaware, The Empire, The Enterprise and The Equitable. Later the Ideal Pottery was erected.

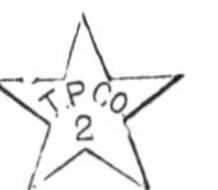


The mark used by the consolidated company is a star. The numeral in the star indicates the plant where the ware was produced, as 1, Crescent; 2, Delaware; 3, Empire; 4, Enterprise; 5, Equitable; 6, Ideal. For example, the plain star enclosing the initials T. P. Co., and the number, 2, was used on the regular sanitary ware of the Delaware Pottery. On all vitreous goods made since 1892 at this establishment is placed a circle surrounding the star, with the name of the ware.

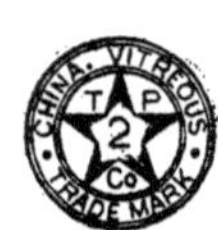


A similar mark, bearing the figure 3, is used on vitreous ware of the Empire plant.

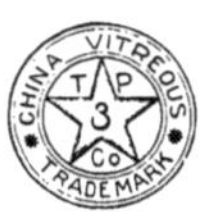

On the sanitary ware of the Enterprise Pottery since 1892 the plain star appears, while on vitreous china the mark is similar to the above with the figure 4 substituted.

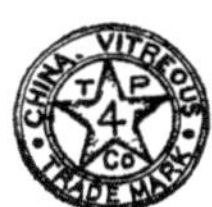


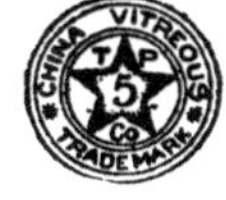


The same mark, with the figure 5 in the star, is used on ware produced at the Equitable plant.

The mark of the Ideal Pottery bears the name instead of a number.

T
IDEAL
P Co

An exhibit was sent to the Paris Exposition of 1900 by The Trenton Potteries Co., which was awarded two gold medals. The pieces were marked with the company's name and address.

TRENTON POTTERIES CO
TRENTON, NEW JERSEY.
U S A

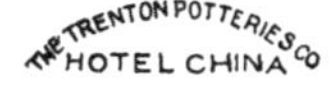


The Crescent Pottery, operated by The Trenton Potteries Co., in 1896 used on Hotel china a similar mark with the name of the consolidated company in full.

In 1891, the initials only were used on vitreous china dinner ware, both thick and thin, produced at the Crescent plant.

T.P.Co.
CHINA

---

## THE BELLMARK POTTERY CO., TRENTON, N. J.

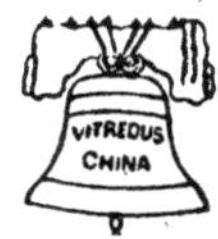


The Bellmark Pottery Co. was formed in 1893. The products are plumbers' and druggists' earthenware. The mark used on these wares is a bell.

## THE FELL & THROPP CO., TRENTON, N. J.

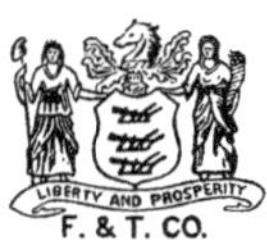


The Fell & Thropp Co. operated the old Taylor & Speeler pottery, known as the Trenton Pottery. It was, until a few years ago, owned by Samuel E. Thropp and J. Hart Brewer, the products being C. C. and white granite wares.

The marks are the Arms of New Jersey. On white granite ware, the British Arms. A tiger's head.

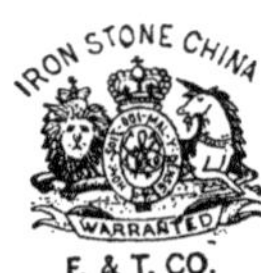

## THE TRENTON POTTERY WORKS, TRENTON, N. J.

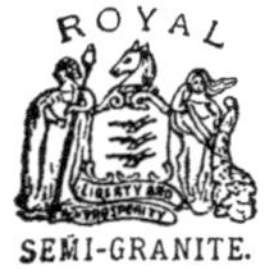


The marks of the Trenton Pottery Works are, for semi-granite or white granite, the Arms of the State of New Jersey.

For opaque porcelain a shield with crossed swords and drapery.

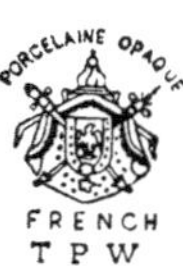


## THE KEYSTONE POTTERY CO., TRENTON, N. J.

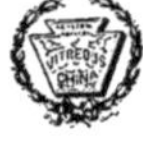

The Keystone Pottery Co. manufactures vitreous china sanitary ware and specialties, which are marked with a keystone enclosed in a wreath.

## THE STAR PORCELAIN CO., TRENTON, N. J.

The Star Porcelain Co., of Trenton, manufactures electrical specialties in porcelain, employing the marks shown here. About one-half of the product, however, is not so marked, but is stamped with the numbers and names of the parties for whom the goods are made.

STAR

---

## THE CERAMIC ART COMPANY, TRENTON, N. J.

The Ceramic Art Co. came into existence in Trenton in 1889, with Jonathan Coxon, Sr., president, and Walter D. Lenox, secretary and treasurer. Their products have always been fine art wares in Belleek and other bodies, either decorated artistically by the best painters or produced in the white state for amateur and professional decorators. The marks which have been used by this company at different times, which are transferred to the ware from copperplates, are as follows:

On undecorated pieces, the initials of the Company and a painter's palette, printed in purple and other colors.

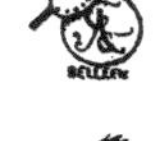

On undecorated ware, called "Indian China," previous to 1895, an Indian's head.

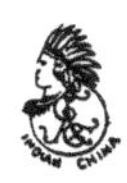


On special decorative work for the trade, a wreath enclosing the full name of the Company.

A special mark, on ware for decorators, used in 1897.

On decorated ware at the present time, a wreath enclosing the Company's initials.

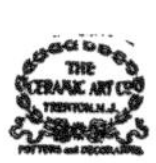


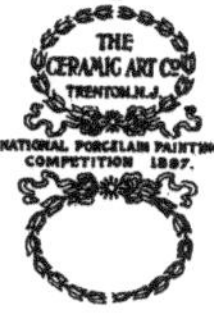


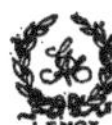

Mr. Lenox is now president of the company. Their most recent productions are overglaze flower designs on Belleek vases and lamps, mounted in gold-plated metal.

---

## THE TRENTON CHINA CO., TRENTON, N. J.

The Trenton China Co. was started in 1859. One of their special productions was a fine grade of vitrified china, white and decorated. This pottery was closed in 1891.

TRENTON CHINA CO.
TRENTON, N.J.

The accompanying mark was *impressed* on table ware.

---

## THE AMERICAN ART CHINA WORKS, TRENTON, N. J.

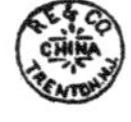


The American Art China Works of Messrs. Rittenhouse, Evans & Co. were established in Trenton in 1891. Their specialty was a thin art ware called American china, plain white and decorated.

---

## COLUMBIAN ART POTTERY, TRENTON, N. J.

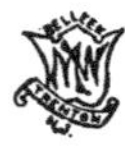

During the year of the World's Columbian Exposition at Chicago, Messrs. Morris & Willmore established the Columbian Art Pottery, at Trenton, for the manufacture of table and toilet china and art wares in Belleek body.

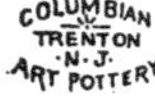


The shield mark is *printed* on Belleek porcelain. The name of the company appears on other wares. On some of their specialties, such as toby jugs in Belleek body and also in opaque china, a miniature copy of the old Liberty bell in Independence Hall, Philadelphia, and other souvenir pieces, the names of customers are also occasionally printed.

## THE AMERICAN PORCELAIN MANUFACTURING CO., GLOUCESTER, N. J.

The American Porcelain M'f'g Co. produced soft porcelain from 1854 to 1857. Their mark consisted of the initials of the company *impressed* in the paste. Marked pieces that are known are embellished with raised floral designs in white. A cream pitcher in the Pennsylvania Museum is decorated with roses, evidently produced in a mold. The pattern has been copied from an English design, which occurs in Parian ware.

A.P.M. Co

---

## L. B. BEERBOWER & CO., ELIZABETH, N. J.

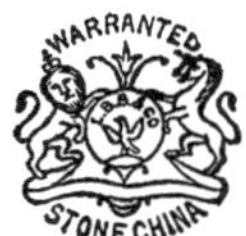


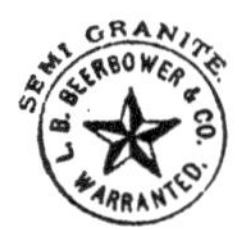


Messrs. L. B. Beerbower & Co. have operated the old pottery at Elizabeth, N. J., for a number of years. These works were established about 1816 for the manufacture of stoneware. Later it was run by a Mr. Pruden, who made yellow and Rockingham wares. The products of the present company are ironstone china, semi-granite, cream-colored and print-decorated wares.

---

## CHAS. WINGENDER & BRO., HADDONFIELD, N. J.

Charles Wingender & Bro. are among the few potters in the United States who continue to produce the old-fashioned German gray stoneware with cobalt blue decorations and salt glaze.

Their beer steins, jardinières, pedestals, water coolers and toby jugs are made after the old German forms, and compare favorably both in decoration and in mechanical execution with the imported ware of a similar nature. This pottery has been operated for about eight years by the Wingender brothers, who came to this country from Germany, where they learned the business. Their ware is sometimes, but not always, stamped with the initials of the firm. The illustration shows a quartette of stoneware mugs with blue foliated decorations and the notation and words of a four-part college

C.W. & BRO.

song. On the reverse side is the name of the owner, in musical characters. A fuller sketch of this pottery will be found in "Pottery and Porcelain of the United States," second edition.

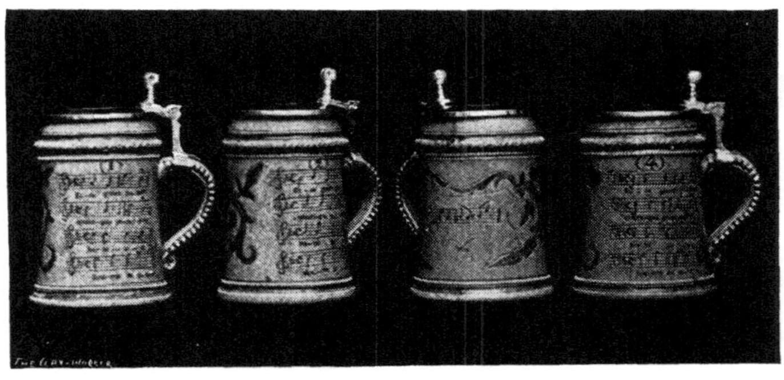

19. Stoneware Mugs.
Charles Wingender & Bro., Haddonfield, N. J.

## WOODBRIDGE, N. J.

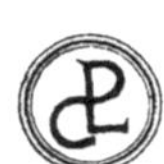

C. L. & H. A. Poillon have recently established an art pottery at Woodbridge, N. J. They manufacture earthenware, decorated with majolica colors; also a fine gold lustre, orange lustre and some matt glazes. They have also produced some colored bodies. One of their specialties is garden pottery, with bold carvings in relief. The mark is the monogram of Clara L. Poillon. This is also used without the circle.

## CHINA DECORATORS IN TRENTON, N. J.

Among the decorating shops of Trenton are those of the Tatler Decorating Co., Jesse Dean, and George Tunnicliffe, whose names are frequently found on examples of their work.

# NEW YORK POTTERIES

# NEW YORK.

## REMMEY & CROLIUS, NEW YORK, N. Y.

ONE of the earliest stoneware potteries in America was that established in New York by John Remmey, a German, about 1735. This factory was situated at "Potter's Hill," near the old City Hall. On an old map showing the plan of New York City in 1742, the pottery of

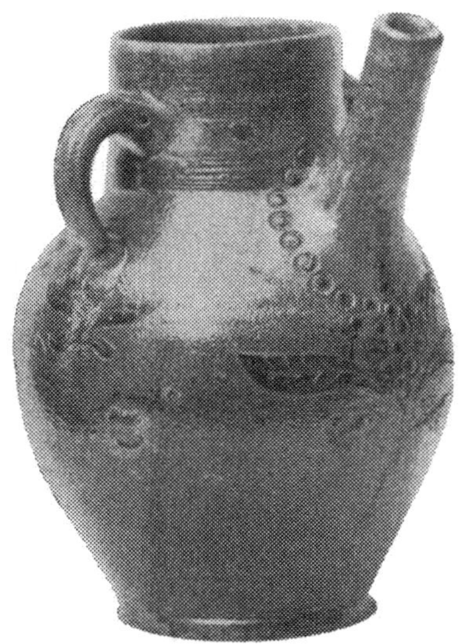

20. Stoneware Jug.
Crolius Pottery, New York, 1798.
By permission of the Editor of *Old China*.

Remmey & Crolius is marked. At a later period, John Remmey having died in 1762, the second partner seems to have been in business alone, as indicated by a jug which is owned by Mrs. L. B. Caswell, Jr., of Fort Atkinson, Wis. This interesting piece, here figured, is a jug eleven inches in height, with two loop handles and a spout. The ware is of a rich brown color, with blue decorations. On the side opposite the spout is the inscription:

New York, Feby 17th, 1798
Flowered by
Mr. Clarkson Crolius.

Around the spout is a conventional design of leaves and flowers, while similar embellishments adorn the body above the inscription.

This pottery continued in operation until about 1820.

---

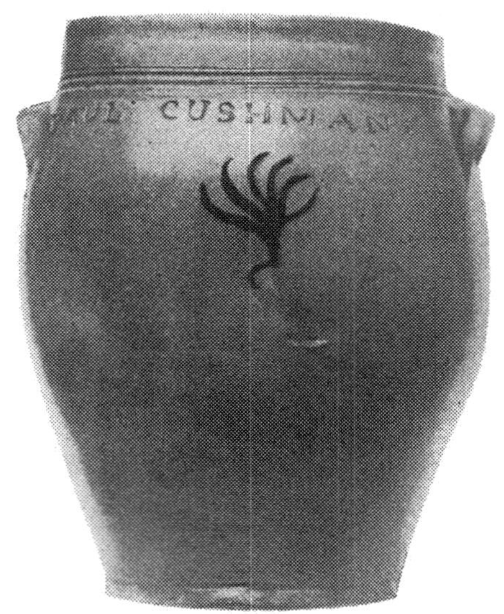


21. Large Stoneware Jar. By Paul Cushman.
Albany, N. Y., about 1809.
In the Pennsylvania Museum.

## PAUL CUSHMAN, ALBANY, N. Y.

About the beginning of the nineteenth century Paul Cushman began the manufacture of salt glazed stoneware, and numerous examples of his work have survived which bear the date 1809. These pieces are principally large jars and crocks, of various shapes. The body is of a brownish tint and the embellishments, which are usually scanty, are in cobalt blue. In many instances the name of the maker is incised on the side, instead of in the bottom, and occasionally other inscriptions are found (see illustration 21).

---

## THE CENTRAL NEW YORK POTTERY, UTICA, N. Y.

A good grade of stoneware is made at the Utica Pottery, which was established about 1828. The ware is salt glazed, but is of a somewhat lighter color than the ordinary German stoneware. The decorations are in a variety of colorings, blue, green, brown, etc., and frequently the ornamentation is in relief. Among the great variety of forms produced at this establishment are ice-water jars, tankards and beer mugs with metal lids. The only marks on this ware that we have seen are stamped numbers, of conspicuous size, which indicate the capacity or dimensions, by which the products of this pottery can be readily distinguished from the German wares. The White family has been connected with these works almost uninterruptedly from the beginning to the present time. The present style is White's Pottery.

---

## SALAMANDER WORKS, NEW YORK, N. Y.

About 1848 the Salamander Works were established in New York City, for the manufacture of flower-pots, milk pans, jugs and other household ware. According to the New York directories, from 1848 to 1855, these works were situated at 54 Cannon Street, and in the years 1848 and 1849, the additional address, 33 West Cannon Street, appears,

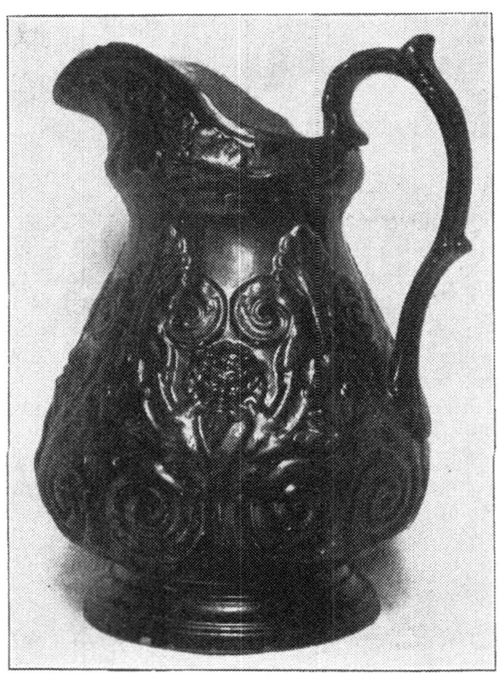

22. Jug with Relief Decorations, Fauns' Heads and Grapes.
Salamander Works, New York, about 1850.
In the Pennsylvania Museum.

showing that in the early years of this pottery salesrooms were occupied in the near vicinity of the works. Little is known of the history of this establishment, but it is believed to have continued in operation until after the breaking out of the Civil War. The ware produced there was of a yellowish or grayish pottery body, with a brown glaze of excellent quality. A pitcher or jug in the collection of the Pennsylvania Museum, Philadelphia, is embellished with relief designs consisting of scroll-work, grapes and leaves, with well-modeled fauns' faces or masks, arranged at regular intervals around the body. The glaze is of a rich, reddish-brown tint, blending into a greenish shade near the base. In modeling, potting and glazing this piece is fully equal to the best ware of that period produced in this country.

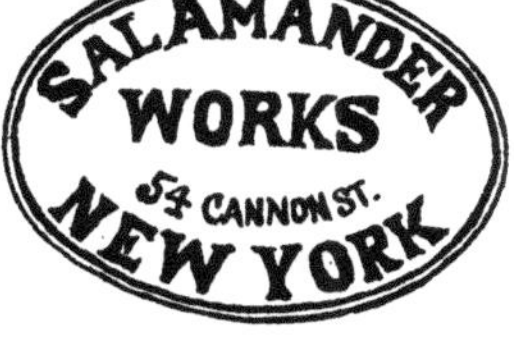


The mark, which is nearly three inches in width, is an oval enclosing the words "Salamander Works, 54 Cannon Street, New York," in large type, impressed in the clay.

---

## THE NEW YORK CITY POTTERY.

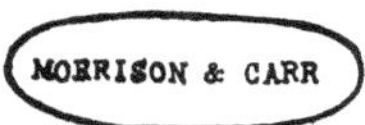


Messrs. Morrison & Carr established a pottery in New York City in 1853. The accompanying mark, *impressed,* is found on some small sauce plates decorated with a magenta margin and gold lines, made in 1860. The ware is white granite of superior quality for that period. This partnership was dissolved in 1871. The first mark used by Mr. Carr alone was the British lion and unicorn, with his initials between. This is often found on decorated white granite ware (see illustration 23).

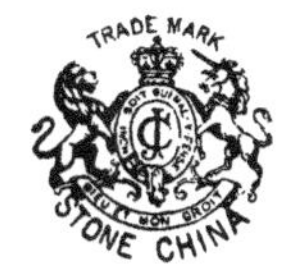


In the last-named year a special stamp was used on sanitary ware and interior car fittings made for the firm of James L. Howard & Co., of Hartford, Conn. This special manufacture extended over a number of years.

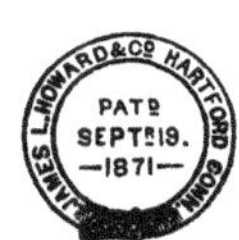


In 1879, Mr. Carr bought the old Speeler Pottery at Trenton, and took into partnership Edward Clark, of Burslem,

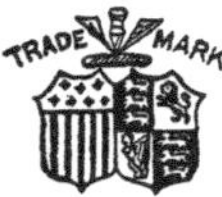


England, under the name of the Lincoln Pottery Co. They began the manufacture of cream-colored and white granite wares and used a mark composed of the American and British shields. Mr. Carr retired from the Trenton establishment after a few months, but continued to use the same mark on cream-colored ware at the New York City Pottery (see International Pottery, Trenton).

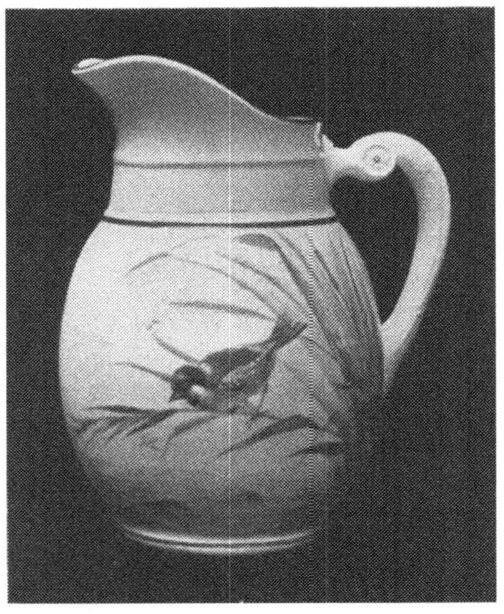

23. **White Ware Pitcher. Overglaze Decoration in Colors. By James Carr, New York. In the Pennsylvania Museum.**

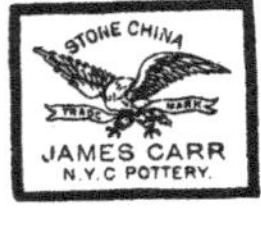


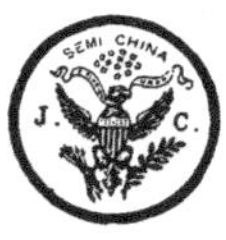


Other marks were used there at various times, until the closing of the works in 1888. On stone china the device was an eagle over the name of the manufacturer and the pottery. On semi-china the mark was a spread-eagle, with the letters J. C. at either side. The device adopted for stone porcelain was the name of the ware and the maker's initials. Another mark employed was composed of clasped hands between the letters J. C. and N. Y. C. P. below. Hotel china was marked with a simple monogram formed of the initials J. C.

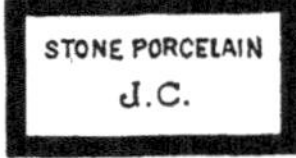


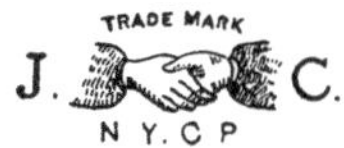


Mr. Carr produced a variety of wares and bodies during the thirty-five years of the New York City Pottery's existence, among which were majolica and Parian, of excellent quality and artistic workmanship. He employed some of the best decorators that could be procured.

A representative collection of Mr. Carr's various products may be seen in the Pennsylvania Museum. Many of these were prepared for the Centennial exhibition, including majolica, Parian, white granite, jet and blue glazed wares, painted plaques and pate-sur-pate work.

Mr. Carr died January 31, 1904, at the age of eighty-four.

---

## CHARLES CARTLIDGE & CO., GREENPOINT, N. Y.

A factory was established by Charles Cartlidge at Greenpoint, L. I., in 1848, and remained in operation until 1856. The bulk of the product of these works was bone porcelain, the composition generally used being five parts of clay (china and blue), two parts of feldspar and four parts of bone. Toward the last a body was successfully made without bone. The ware is characterized by translucency and a yellowish-white tint of the paste. Table ware, Parian portrait busts, porcelain hardware, buttons, ornamental figures and a multiplicity of objects, useful and ornamental, were produced in quantities. The best china painters were employed in decorating the wares. It is not known that any factory marks were used, at least none have been found on those pieces that have been fully identified. A representative series of Cartlidge porcelain may be seen in the American collection of the Pennsylvania Museum, procured mainly from some of the descendants of the founder of the works.

## THE UNION PORCELAIN WORKS, GREENPOINT, N. Y.

The Union Porcelain Works were established by some German potters previous to the breaking out of the Civil War. They were soon after purchased by Thomas C. Smith, whose son, C. H. L. Smith, yet continues to operate them. This is one of the few American potteries which have engaged in the manufacture of hard porcelain.

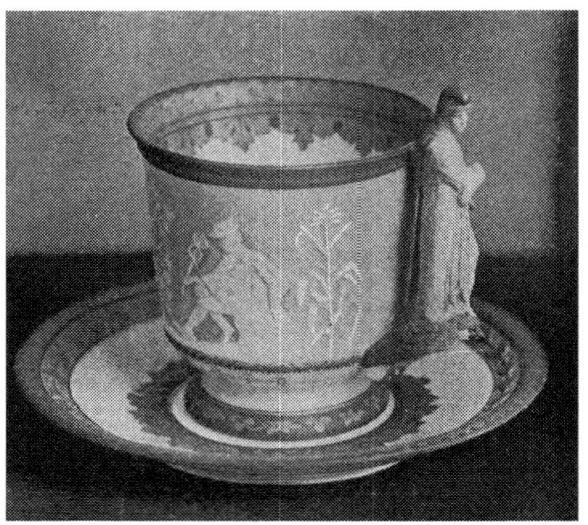

24. "Liberty" Cup, in Hard Paste.
Union Porcelain Works, Greenpoint, N. Y.

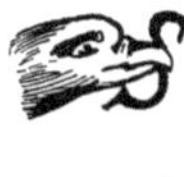

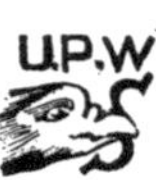


In 1876 they first began using a mark—an eagle's head with letter S in beak. This was *impressed* in hard porcelain table ware. In 1877 the same device was printed in green beneath the glaze. Since that date the mark has been used in conjunction with the initials U. P. W. In some instances the same device has been applied as a raised tablet on large pieces and also on small relief portrait medallions. Since 1879 a decorating-shop mark has been used on overglaze painted pieces. It is usually printed in red above the glaze and sometimes has the date of manufacture placed below. Later this mark was modified by the omission of the word "Greenpoint." In August, 1891, a semi-circular decorating mark was adopted, which has been used until the present time.

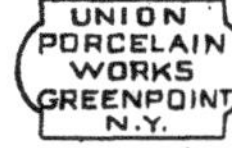


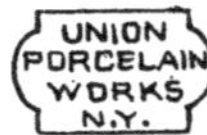


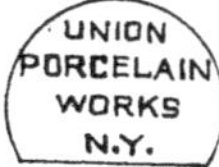


## THE ONONDAGA POTTERY CO., SYRACUSE, N. Y.

In 1871, The Onondaga Pottery Co. was organized, for the manufacture of white granite ware. The Arms of New York State was the mark on this grade of ware, from 1874 to 1893, when its manufacture was discontinued. From 1890 to 1893 the "Imperial Geddo" mark was used, on the first china ware made by this company. In the latter year a new mark was substituted for this ware and discontinued in 1895. From that date until 1897 the globe mark was employed.

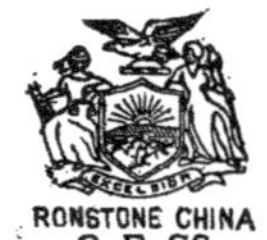


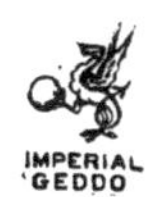


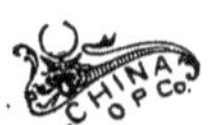


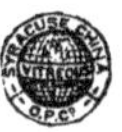


Semi-porcelain ware, from 1886 to 1898, was marked "Semi-Vitreous," and since 1897 the "Syracuse China" mark has been in use.

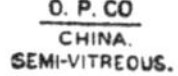


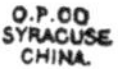


Mrs. Adelaide Alsop-Robineau has recently been decorating porcelain hotel ware in underglaze designs for this company. Her work is marked with her initials. Mrs. Robineau stands among the foremost decorators in the National League of Mineral Painters, and her work is original as well as of a high order of merit.

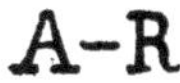

## VOLKMAR POTTERY.

Charles Volkmar began making vases and tiles with underglaze decorations at Greenpoint, N. Y., about 1879, and the mark used from that date until 1888 was his monogram.

In 1895 Mr. Volkmar organized the Volkmar Keramic Co., in Brooklyn, N. Y., for the manufacture of Volkmar tiles. He produced a series of plaques with underglaze blue designs of historical buildings and American portraits. The

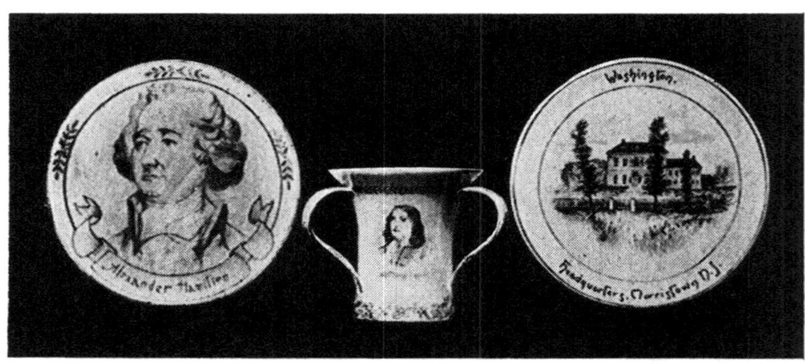

25. Volkmar and Cory Pottery. Corona, N. Y.
Alexander Hamilton Plaque. William Penn Loving Cup.
Washington's Headquarters at Morristown, N. J.

VOLKMAR

mark which he employed was the name "Volkmar" in raised letters in an impressed parallelogram. Later in the same year he formed a partnership with Miss Kate Cory, and moved the works to Corona, N. Y., continuing the manufacture of these plaques. The decorations were painted in blue beneath the glaze, principally by Miss Cory, a competent artist. Among the best examples of her work are a plaque with portrait of Alexander Hamilton, a William Penn loving cup and a series of plates showing the different headquarters of General Washington. The mark at that time was the firm name impressed (see illustration 25).

VOLKMAR & CORY

Since 1896 his ware has been principally in plain colored glazes, and the mark used is the initial of his last name, either in relief or incised in the green clay.

V.

In 1903, Charles Volkmar & Son erected a pottery at Metuchen, N. J., where they are now manufacturing a line of art ware, principally in matt enamels on a semi-stone body. The latter mark is yet used, being scratched with a point in the wet clay.

---

## EAST MORRISANIA CHINA WORKS, NEW YORK

These works were started by Mr. D. Robitzek on 150th Street, for the production of porcelain door knobs and hardware trimmings. The present products are white granite, cream-colored and decorated wares.

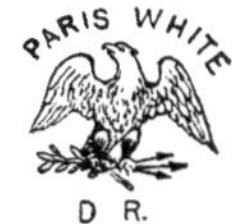


---

## THE FAIENCE MANUFACTURING CO., GREENPOINT, N. Y.

The Faience Manufacturing Co., of New York and Brooklyn, established an art pottery at Greenpoint, Long Island, in 1880, where, during the next ten years or so, some of the most artistic wares, in white faience and hard porcelain bodies, that have ever been produced in this country were made. The shapes were original and handsome, and the decorations were painted by the best artists. An incised mark, composed of the initial letters of the company's name, was used on some of the earlier products, such as "majolica" and so-termed "barbotine" wares.

FMC

On changing from coarse faience to finer grades of goods the name of the company seemed inappropriate, and so it was proposed to adopt the name "Royal Crown" ware for their improved china bodies, to cater to the public taste, which, at that time, demanded "Royal" wares. This mark was, however, used but a short time and on but a few lots of ware. It was printed beneath the glaze.

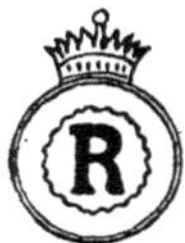

The mark used on decorated faience, between 1886 and 1892, was the monogram of the company, which was penciled in black, green, etc., above the glaze (see illustration 26). Other marks which appear on pieces are numbers which re-

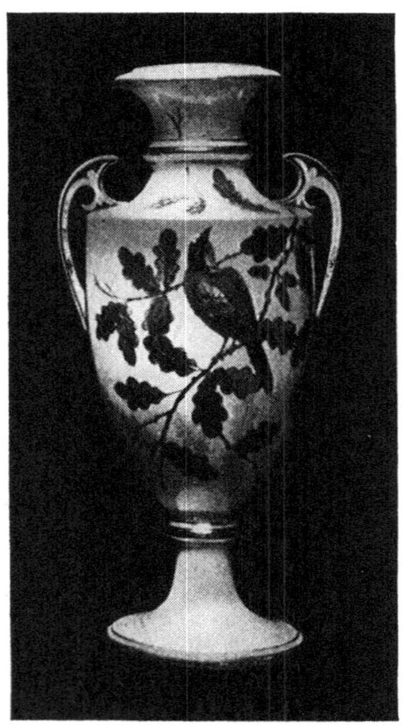

26. White Faience Vase. Decorations in Colors and Raised Gold.
Faience Manufacturing Co., Greenpoint, N. Y.
In the Pennsylvania Museum.

late to the shapes and decorations. The factory was closed in the last-named year.

Mr. Edward Lycett, now residing in Atlanta, Ga., was superintendent and principal decorator of the works, and many of the most artistic shapes were designed by him. He also compounded some of their best bodies, including a true hard paste porcelain, which was used in the later days for the best vase forms, many of which possessed perforated covers, necks and handles.

## THE CHARLES GRAHAM CHEMICAL POTTERY WORKS, BROOKLYN, N. Y.

The Charles Graham Chemical Pottery Works have produced some artistic varieties of stoneware, the work of Mr.

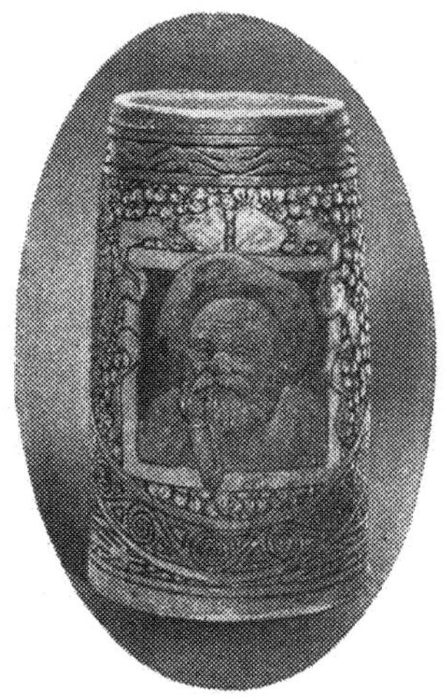

27. Stoneware Mug. Carved Decorations.
Executed by Charles C. Benham.
By courtesy of *The Ladies' Home Journal.*

Chas. C. Benham, who has been experimenting in carving and coloring designs in this body for twenty-five years. The mark on beer mugs and other small pieces is *impressed.*

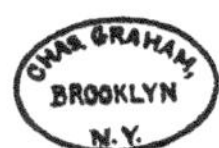

## EAST HAMPTON AND WEST HAMPTON, N. Y.

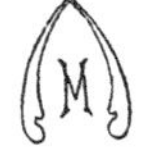


The Middle Lane Pottery, erected at East Hampton, Long Island, was established by Mr. T. A. Brouwer, Jr., a few years ago, where he turned out some of the most beautiful metallic lustre effects thus far produced in this country. The mark consists of the outlines of the jaw bones of a whale, with the letter M, the initial of the name of the potttery, in the centre. The design was suggested by the arched entrance to the grounds which was formed by the jaw-bones of a colossal whale that was washed ashore at this point some years ago.

The products and peculiar glaze effects of the Middle Lane Pottery are what the inventor calls "Fire Painting," "Iridescent Fire Work," "Gold Leaf Underglaze," "Sea Grass" and "Flame," produced by various treatments, through the action of the fire. The mark is *impressed*.

Recently Mr. Brouwer has moved his pottery to West Hampton, where he has erected a new and exceedingly novel building, in the form of a miniature castle. The name has been changed to the Brouwer Pottery. Only hard body and glazes are now used, and the time of firing by Mr. Brouwer's peculiar process has been reduced to about six hours, while only about one hour is required for the glazing. Pieces produced at the West Hampton works also bear the signature of the maker.

---

## THE CHITTENANGO POTTERY CO., CHITTENANGO, N. Y.

CHINA
C. P. CO.

Operations were commenced by this company in 1897. The products are decorated and undecorated china.

This company received the contract for furnishing souvenir china for the Buffalo Exhibition. The marks are here shown.

C. P. Co.
CHINA

C. P. Co.
CHITTENANGO, N.Y.
CHINA

## THE AMERICAN ART CERAMIC CO., CORONA, N. Y.

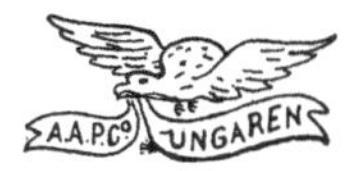


The American Art Pottery Co. was started recently at Corona, Long Island, for the manufacture of artistic terra-cotta and pottery. In the latter part of 1901 the company was incorporated under the name of the American Art Ceramic Co. The word "Ungaren" in the mark is the German for Hungary.

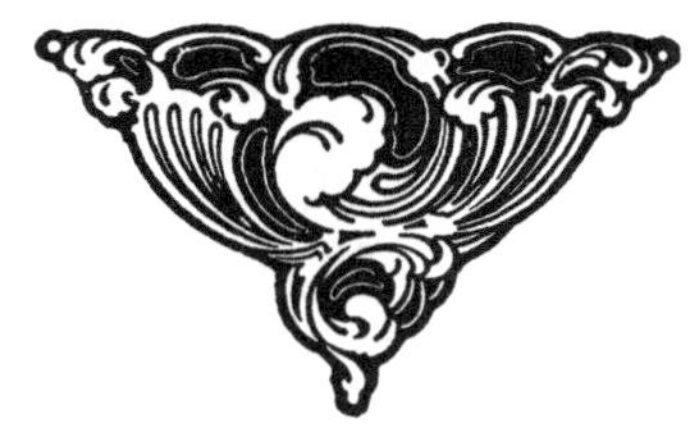

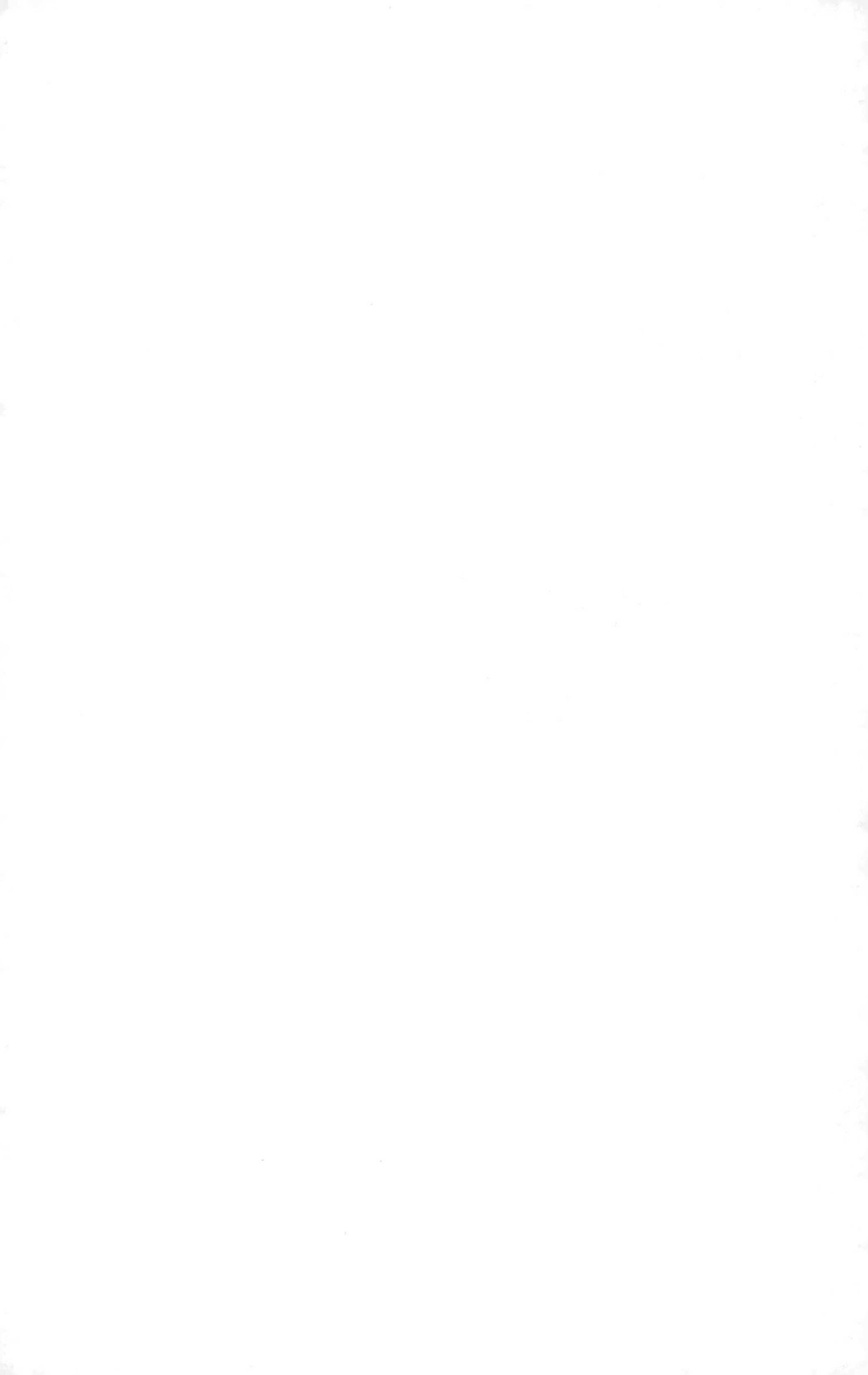

# NEW ENGLAND POTTERIES

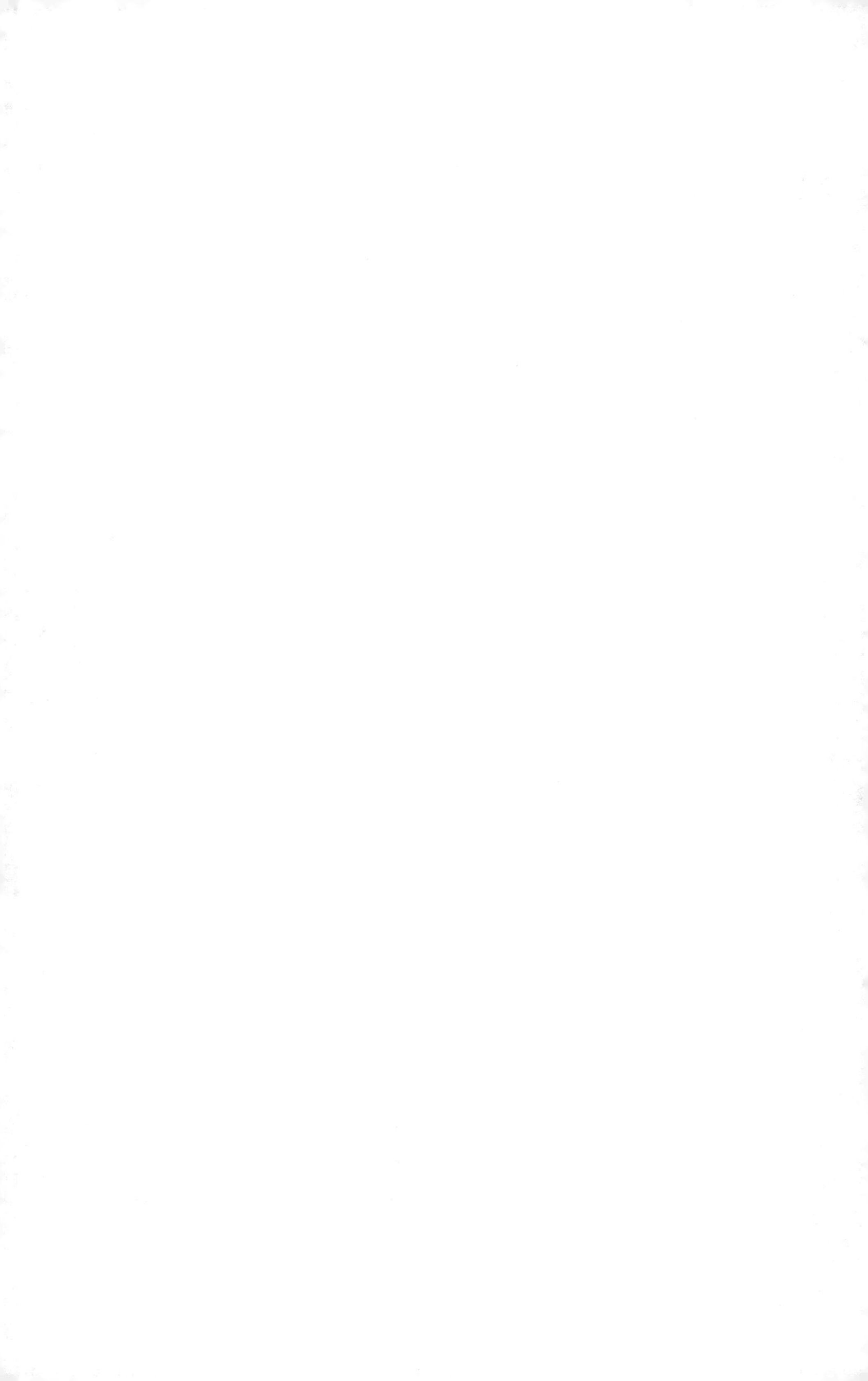

# NEW ENGLAND.

## BENNINGTON, VERMONT.

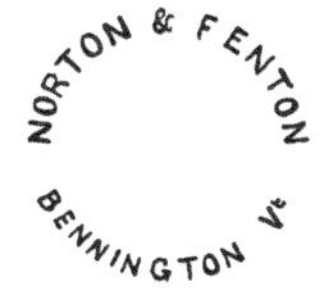


THE Norton Pottery was established at Bennington, Vt., in 1793. At a later date (about 1839) Christopher Weber Fenton became a member of the firm. They made stoneware and brown glazed pottery. A large brown water pitcher, in the Pennsylvania Museum, bearing the Norton & Fenton mark, *impressed,* is decorated with relief designs of roses and scroll-work. This mark is two and a quarter inches in diameter (see illustration 28).

E. & L. P. Norton took the pottery about 1865 and continued it until 1882, when the style became E. Norton & Co. Salt glazed stoneware was the principal product.

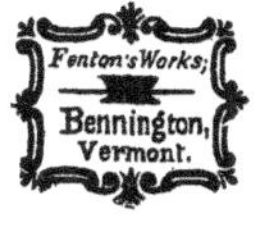


A mark, consisting of a raised panel in which are *impressed* the words "Fenton's Works, Bennington, Vermont," was used on pieces of Parian ware produced about 1845, the first Parian to be made in the United States, some three years after its first appearance in England. Mr. Fenton, at this period, appears to have been in business alone. A pitcher so marked, is decorated with relief designs of knights in armor and on the reverse side with a lady on horseback and a harper. This piece appears to have been copied from a design produced by S. Alcock & Co., of Burslem, Staffordshire (see illustration 29).

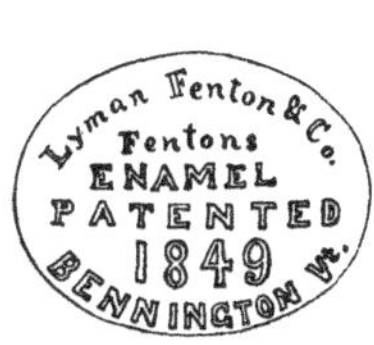


The firm of Lyman, Fenton & Co. came into existence about 1848 or 1849. One of their specialties was the "Patent Flint Enameled" ware, a fine grade of Rockingham. The mark used on this variety of ware was a large ellipse, nearly three inches in width, enclosing the inscription "Lyman, Fenton & Co. Fenton's Enamel, Patented 1849. Bennington, Vt." (see illustration 30). Being *impressed* in the ware, which is often uncolored on the bottom, this mark is fre-

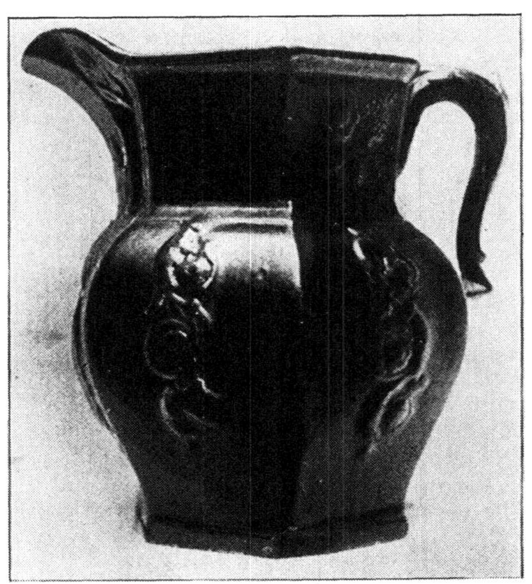

28. Brown Glazed Pitcher. Relief Decoration.
By Norton and Fenton,
Bennington, Vt., about 1840.

quently undecipherable, having been almost, or quite, obliterated by the filling in of the glaze. Flint Enameled ware is of three varieties, black and yellow mottled, olive and yellow, and a combination of yellow-brown, dark red, green

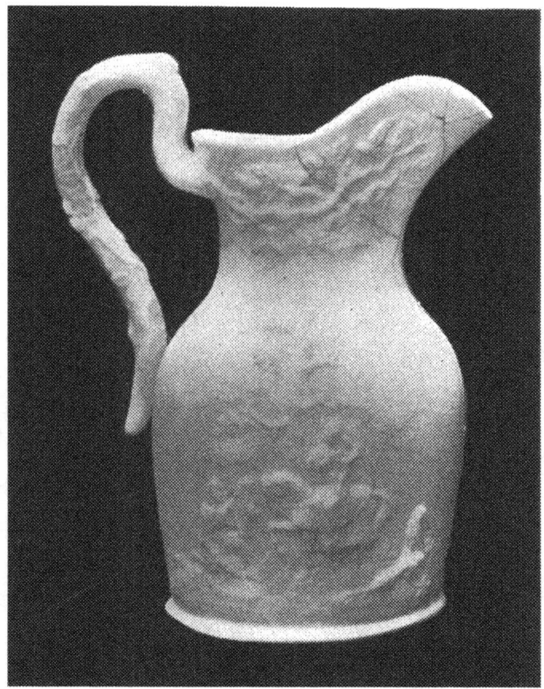

29. Parian Pitcher. Relief Decorations.
Fenton's Works, Bennington, Vt., 1845.
In the Pennsylvania Museum.

and blue. These effects are seen to best advantage in picture frames, pitchers, toby jugs and candlesticks. The glaze is often very heavy and far more brilliant than in the ordinary Rockingham ware.

In 1849 new buildings were erected and the style was

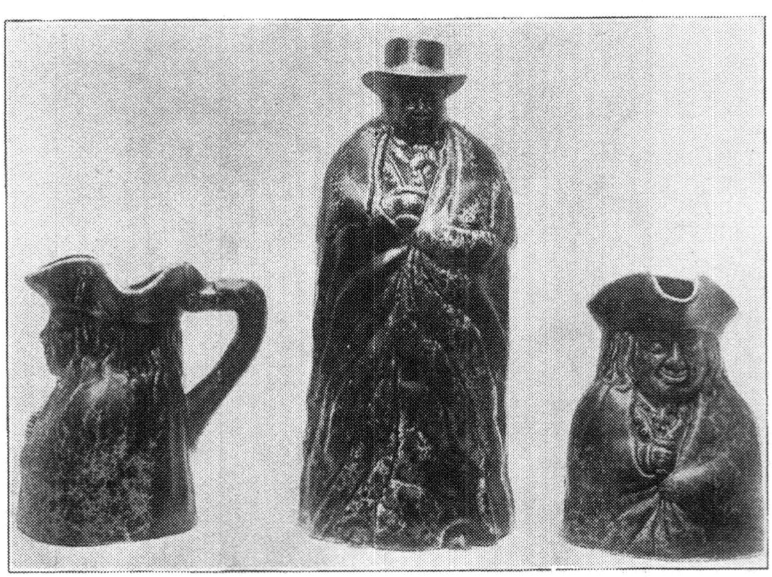

30. Group of "Flint Enamel" Ware.
Toby Jugs and Bottle.
U. S. Pottery, Bennington, Vt., 1849.
In the Pennsylvania Museum.

changed to the United States Pottery Co. Parian ware was made in abundance, and several modelers were employed to originate ornamental designs. Porcelain biscuit toys and figures were also produced in large numbers. The Parian ware was marked with a raised ribbon or scroll bearing the initials of the pottery (U. S. P.) and two variable numbers, indicating the size and shape, or pattern (see illustration 31).

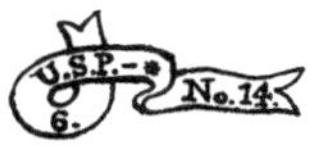


The Parian ware is of two varieties, a grayish-white and pure white. It is either decorated in relief without coloring, or possesses a pitted ground in deep blue, against which the raised white figures appear to good advantage. The pottery was closed in 1858.

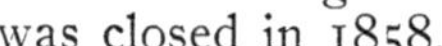

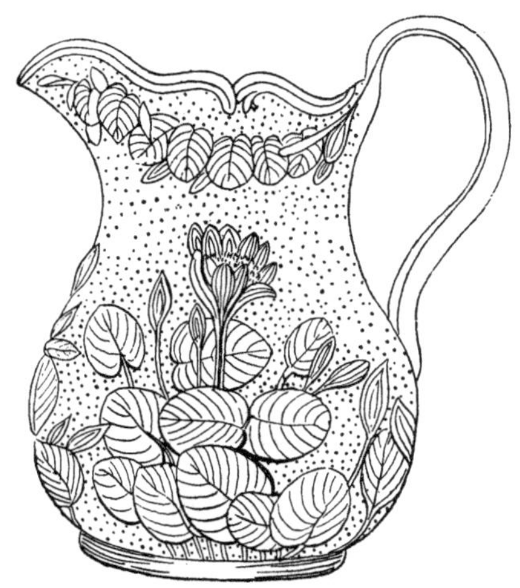

31. Parian Pitcher. Water Lily Decoration in Relief.
U. S. Pottery Co.
Bennington, Vt., about 1856.

Other marks, found on different wares, are an ellipse enclosing the words "United States Pottery, Bennington, Vt.," *impressed,* usually placed on "lava," "scrodled," or marbled ware, and a relief label, of diamond shape, bearing the same lettering, also *impressed,* which occurs on porcelain or semi-porcelain. A large pitcher, modeled to represent the falling water of a cataract, bears the latter mark. An example may be seen in the Pennsylvania Museum.

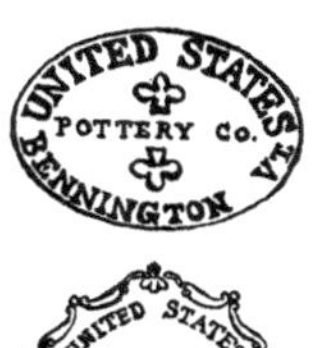

## NICHOLS & ALFORD, BURLINGTON, VT.

Nichols & Alford
Manufacturers
1854
Burlington, Vt.

This firm was manufacturing earthenware in Burlington, Vt., in the year 1854, as is indicated by a brown-glazed, hound-handled pitcher bearing the annexed mark. It is said that some of the molds used here were obtained from the Bennington pottery, and it is probable that some of the workmen from the latter establishment went to Burlington. This firm also produced Rockingham ware and stoneware.

---

## NEW ENGLAND POTTERY CO.

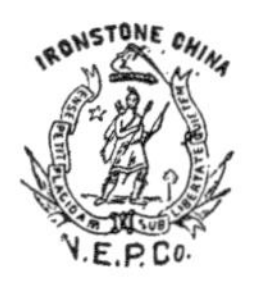


A pottery was established in East Boston, Mass., in 1854, by Frederick Meagher, for the manufacture of common white ware. In 1875 Thomas Gray and L. W. Clark took the works, under the name of the New England Pottery Co.

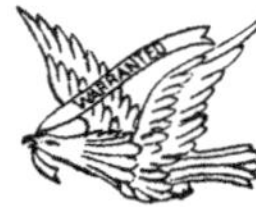

The first mark employed by the company was the great Seal or Arms of the State of Massachusetts, which was used from about 1878 to 1883 on ironstone china or white granite ware.

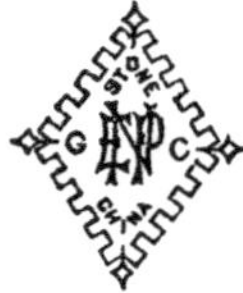
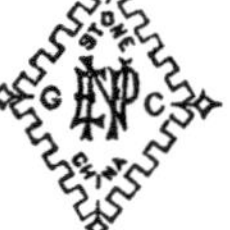

A special order of goods for a private purchaser was marked with a flying eagle. This was printed in black beneath the glaze.

A lozenge-shaped device with meander bordering, enclosing the monogram of the name of the company and initials of the proprietors, was used on stone china from 1883 to 1886.

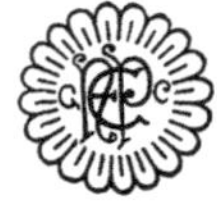

Cream-colored ware has been marked in black with a similar design, having a scalloped, circular outline, from 1887 to the present time.

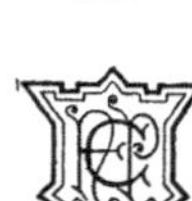
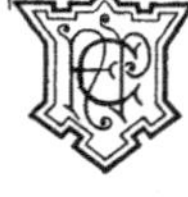

For white granite ware the mark was a shield. This was printed in black, under the glaze, during the years 1886 to 1892, when its manufacture was discontinued.

In 1886 the firm began to make a semi-porcelain ware in colored bodies, which was decorated in an artistic manner. To this product they gave the name of "Rieti" ware. This was first marked in black beneath the glaze, with a mailed hand holding a dagger.

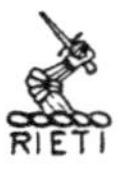

In 1888, the design was changed, and from that date until 1889 the "Rieti" mark was a shell bearing the name, also printed in black beneath the glaze.

From 1889 to 1895, when the production of "Rieti" ware was abandoned, the mark was a crown and shield combined, printed *on* the glaze in red.

The present mark, used on special articles and shapes, in "Paris White" ware, was adopted in 1897.

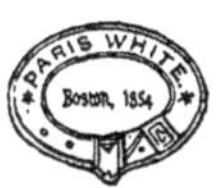


Much of the ware produced at the New England Pottery in the past was of a highly artistic character. Mr. Clark died a few years ago and Mr. Gray is now the sole proprietor.

---

## CHELSEA AND DEDHAM, MASS.

The Chelsea Keramic Art Works were established at Chelsea, Mass., by Alexander W. Robertson in 1866. The wares which have been produced here are mainly reproductions of antique and Oriental potteries and porcelains. Hugh C. Robertson, a son of the founder, has been the leading spirit and is still actively engaged in the work.

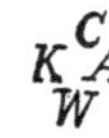


CHELSEA KERAMIC
ART WORKS
ROBERTSON & SONS.

In 1891 a company was incorporated under the name of the "Chelsea Pottery, U. S." About 1896 or 1897 the works were moved to Dedham, Mass., when the title was changed to the Dedham Pottery.

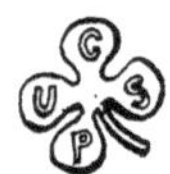


The marks used at various times are as follows: The initials of the Chelsea Keramic Art Works *impressed* in different art wares, from 1875 to 1889. The name of the works, *impressed*, from 1875 to 1880. A four-leaf clover bearing the impressed initials, C. P. U. S., was introduced in 1891, and about two years later an outlined rabbit, foreshortened, was used. Still later, at the Dedham Pottery, a square stamp with the name of the pottery was impressed or printed on various art productions.

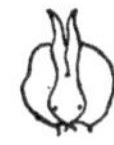

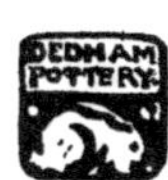


Among Mr. Robertson's more important achievements are his reproductions of the Chinese Dragon's Blood glaze, crackle stoneware with blue inglaze decorations, and heavy, slow-flowing glazes after the old Japanese.

## HAMPSHIRE POTTERY, KEENE, N. H.

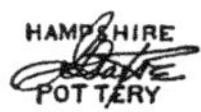

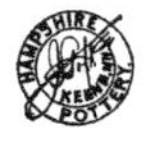

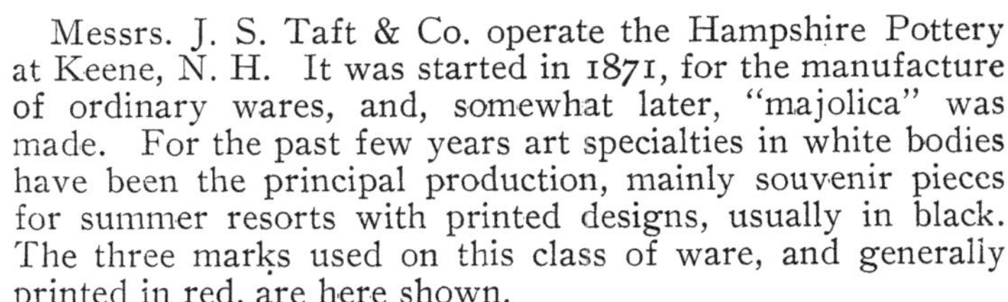

Messrs. J. S. Taft & Co. operate the Hampshire Pottery at Keene, N. H. It was started in 1871, for the manufacture of ordinary wares, and, somewhat later, "majolica" was made. For the past few years art specialties in white bodies have been the principal production, mainly souvenir pieces for summer resorts with printed designs, usually in black. The three marks used on this class of ware, and generally printed in red, are here shown.

---

## NEW MILFORD, CONN.

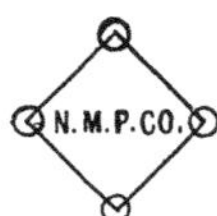


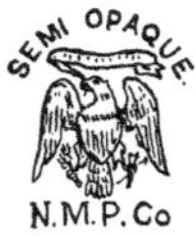


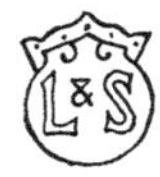


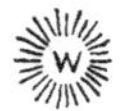


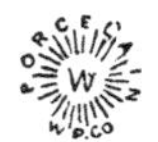


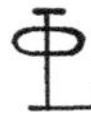

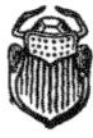

The New Milford Pottery Co. was established as a stock company in 1886. The products were the ordinary grades of white ware. On C. C. goods the mark was a square with the initials of the company's name.

For semi-opaque china the eagle mark was used.

A limited quantity of ware was made for their New York agents, Messrs. Lang & Schafer, on which a circular mark with the firm's initials was placed.

The name of the concern was later changed to The Wannopee Pottery Co., under which title it has since been known. The marks in present use are sun bursts enclosing a W, one used on "Duchess" ware, which is characterized by mottled glazes, and one on porcelain.

The Park Lane Pottery, under the same management, produced a novel ware covered with a metallic glaze, closely resembling copper. The mark is the monogram of the pottery.

The name "Scarabronze" was adopted for this ware, the mark being an Egyptian scarabaeus, either applied somewhere on the surface in relief, or impressed in the base. A few pieces were issued marked with paper labels containing the scarab in gold. The forms of vases are derived from the old Egyptian, and the surface of the metallic glaze is exceedingly smooth and pleasing to the touch. Mr. A. H. Noble, the head of the company, retired from the business in 1903.

Among the products of the Wannopee Pottery are some modeled semi-porcelain pitchers with a "smear" or dull glaze, somewhat resembling in appearance Parian ware. One variety is embellished with relief medallion heads of Beethoven and Mozart. Another bears medallion busts marked "Napoleon." These are white with the exception of a band of leaves in relief around top and base, which in the first mentioned is colored brown, and in the latter a greenish lemon. The ground of these pitchers is coarsely pitted. These cheap affairs, which appeared first in 1895, are sometimes offered by dealers as rare antiques, one of the "Napoleon" jugs having recently been sold to an uninitiated collector for a high price. The modeling is the work of Mr. Victor Gallimore, of Trenton, N. J.

---

## THE GRUEBY FAIENCE CO., BOSTON, MASS.

The Grueby Faience Co. was organized in June, 1897, by Messrs. Grueby, Graves and Kendrick. The ware is a hard, semi-porcelain body, covered with an opaque lustreless enamel, of great smoothness and a satiny finish. The forms of the pieces are derived from the ancient Egyptian, the prevailing color being a cool, cucumber-green, although recently other colors, such as yellow, blue and purple, have been introduced. The marks employed at different times, which are *impressed*, are here shown. The modeled decorations, in low

GRUEBY

GRUEBY POTTERY
BOSTON.U.S.A.

GRUEBY
BOSTON.MASS

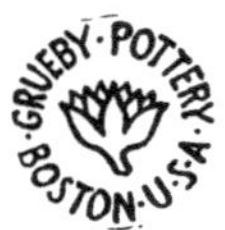


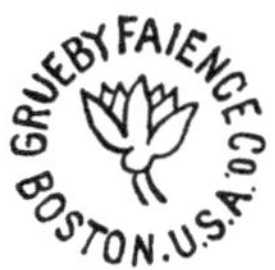

relief, are done entirely by hand, mainly by young women artists, whose initials and monograms are usually found on pieces of their work. They are as follows:

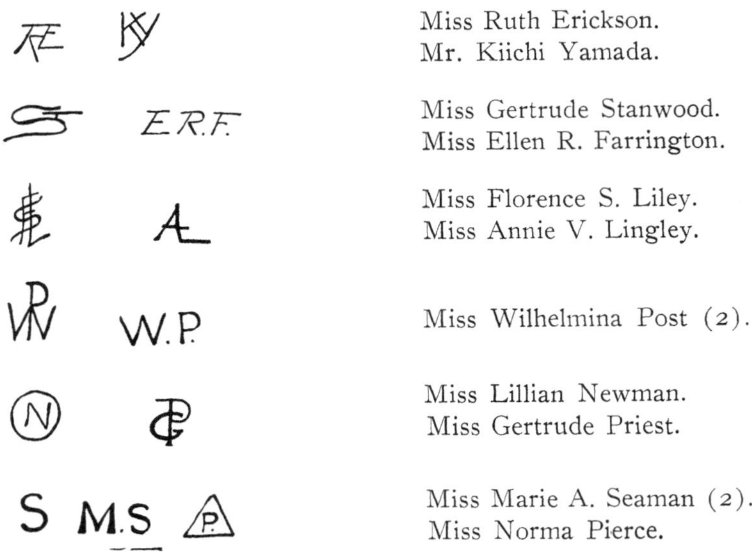

Miss Ruth Erickson.
Mr. Kiichi Yamada.

Miss Gertrude Stanwood.
Miss Ellen R. Farrington.

Miss Florence S. Liley.
Miss Annie V. Lingley.

Miss Wilhelmina Post (2).

Miss Lillian Newman.
Miss Gertrude Priest.

Miss Marie A. Seaman (2).
Miss Norma Pierce.

---

## THE MERRIMAC CERAMIC CO., NEWBURYPORT, MASS.

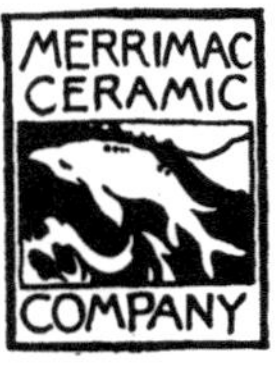


The Merrimac Ceramic Co. has for its leading spirit T. S. Nickerson, who is a member of the Society of Arts and Crafts, Boston. The company was organized in 1897 for the manufacture of cheap florists' wares and enameled tile. For a year or so terra-cotta and enameled pottery have been manufactured. These wares are of decorative quality and the colored glazes are of unusual merit. The principal product at present is house and garden pottery in artistic forms.

A paper label was attached to all pieces made from September, 1900, to August, 1901. Since the latter date, the mark has been *impressed*.

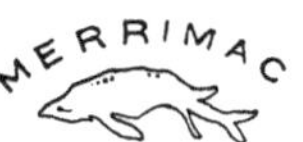


The device is a fish (sturgeon), which is the Indian meaning of Merrimac.

On January 1, 1902, the name was changed to the Merrimac Pottery Co., and the most recent achievements are dull enamels in great variety.

---

## THE LOW ART TILE CO., CHELSEA, MASS.

Arthur Osborne was the chief modeler for the Low Art Tile Co., of Chelsea, Mass., previous to 1893. His mark, found on many tiles and plastic sketches, is his monogram.

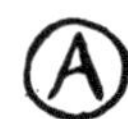


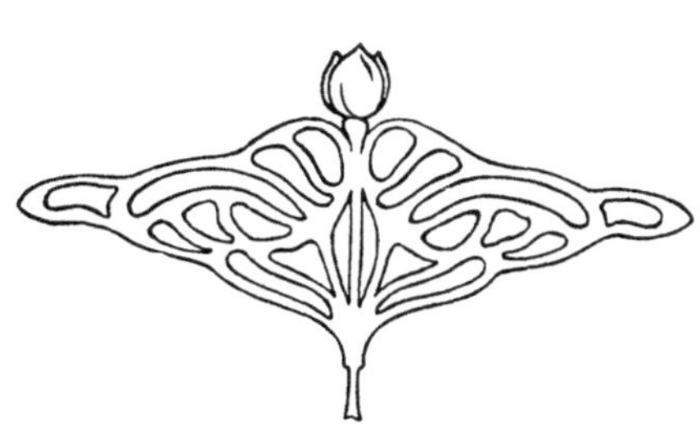

# OHIO POTTERIES

# OHIO.

## THE HARKER POTTERY CO., EAST LIVERPOOL, OHIO.

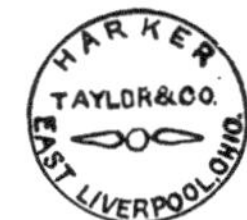


THE Harker Pottery Co. was incorporated in 1890. The business was established by Benjamin Harker, Sr., in 1840, when the manufacture of yellow and Rockingham wares was begun.

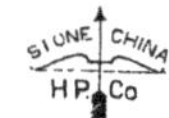


From 1847 to 1850 or later the firm name was Harker, Taylor & Co. They produced Rockingham pieces, such as hunting and hound-handled pitchers, bearing an *embossed* and *impressed* stamp.

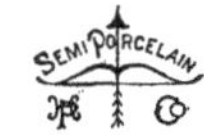


George S. Harker & Co. followed some years later. Since 1879 white granite and semi-porcelain have been the staple products of these works. The two marks here shown,—a bow and arrow with the initials of the company,—have been used for a number of years.

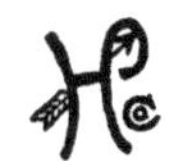

The Harker Pottery Co. at one time decorated the goods made at other potteries, as is shown by a white granite portrait plate bearing the impressed factory mark of Burroughs, Mountford & Co., of Trenton, and the subjoined arrow and monogram device, printed in black. This piece was produced in 1892.

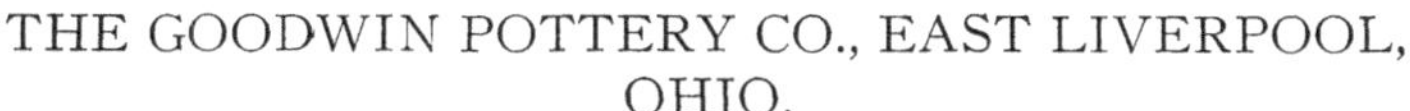

## THE GOODWIN POTTERY CO., EAST LIVERPOOL, OHIO.

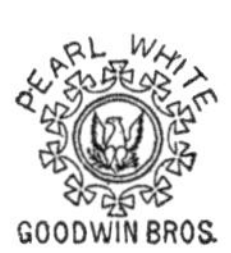


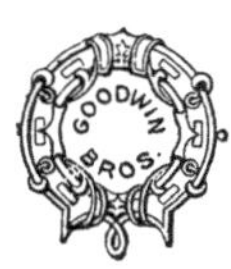


Mr. John Goodwin established a pottery in East Liverpool, Ohio, for the production of yellow and Rockingham wares in 1844. In 1876, after Mr. Goodwin's death, his three sons succeeded him, and in 1893 the Goodwin Pottery Co. was incorporated. Their products are pearl white, cream-colored and decorated wares, semi-porcelain and ironstone china or white granite.

The various marks used by this company are here shown

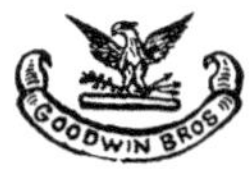


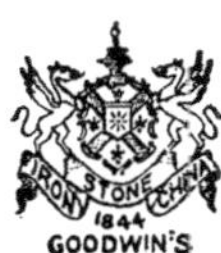


GOODWIN'S
HOTEL CHINA

---

## THE SMITH-PHILLIPS CHINA CO., EAST LIVERPOOL, OHIO.

SMITH-PHILLIPS
HOTEL
CHINA

The Smith-Phillips China Co. manufactures hotel china and semi-porcelain ware.

Mark for hotel china, the firm name in a circle.

KOSMO

FENIX

Marks used on toilet wares of the "Kosmo" and "Fenix" patterns.

Marks used on dinner ware.

AMERICAN GIRL

SMITH PHILLIPS
SEMI PORCELAIN

---

## THE VODREY POTTERY CO., EAST LIVERPOOL, OHIO.

The Vodrey Pottery Co. was incorporated in 1896. Its predecessors were Woodward & Vodrey, who commenced business in 1848; Woodward, Blakeley & Co., 1849; Vodrey & Brother, 1857. The company manufactures white granite and semi-porcelain. The marks used since 1879 are here shown, the first nine being used on dinner ware and the other five on toilet shapes.

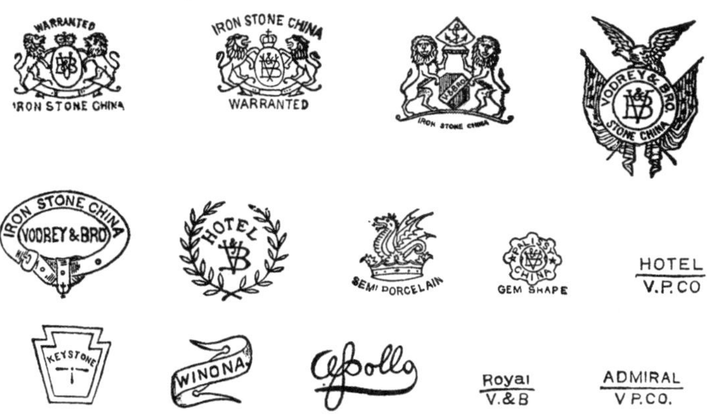


## THE WILLIAM BRUNT POTTERY CO., EAST LIVERPOOL, OHIO.

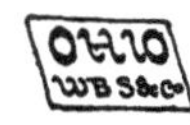


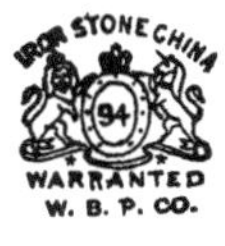


The firm of William Brunt, Son & Co. began business about 1850. The William Brunt Pottery Co. (Phœnix Pottery) was incorporated in 1894. The present products are ironstone china and decorated wares. The marks used before incorporation were a crescent, and a parallelogram enclosing the firm's initials.

The British Arms, with the date of incorporation, was used on white granite.

Other marks, mainly on toilet and table wares, are shown below:

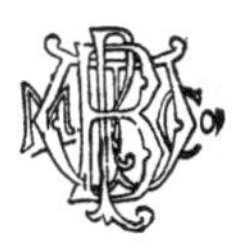

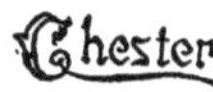


ROCKET

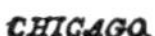


ELECTRIC

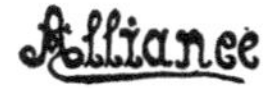

## THE KNOWLES, TAYLOR & KNOWLES CO.

The present pottery plant of The Knowles, Taylor & Knowles Co., of East Liverpool, Ohio, is claimed to be the most extensive in America. The works were established in 1854 by Isaac W. Knowles and Isaac A. Harvey. They began with a single kiln, which they used alternately for firing the body of yellow ware and glazing it. In 1870 Mr. Knowles, who had become the sole proprietor, formed a partnership with Col. John N. Taylor and Homer S. Knowles. Two years later they began the manufacture of white granite ware. In 1888, Joseph G. Lee and Willis A. Knowles were admitted to the firm, and in 1891 a stock company was incorporated under the name of The Knowles, Taylor & Knowles Co. The products of this manufactory have been varied and extensive, the principal being white granite, semi-vitreous porcelain and hotel china. Some of the most artistic ware ever produced in America has been made here. In 1893 they began the manufacture of a fine art porcelain of beautiful Chinese white body and velvety glaze, which they named "Lotus" ware. This was sold principally in the white state for decorating, but was finally abandoned on account of its costliness. At present the company operates more than thirty-five kilns and employs upwards of seven hundred hands.

The marks used at various times since 1872 are as follows:

Bison mark, on white granite or stone china.

Variation of same, on hotel china and white granite.

Same mark, on ironstone or white granite.

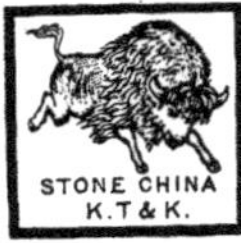


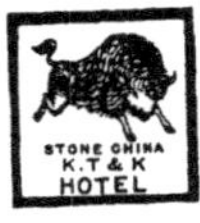


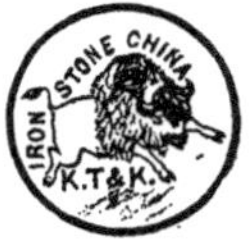

Bison head mark, on stone china or white granite.
Eagle mark, on ironstone china.
Variation of same.
Eagle trade-mark, on ironstone china, 1879.
Variation of same, used in 1881.
Eagle mark, "Warranted Granite."

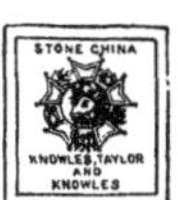

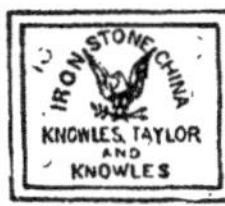

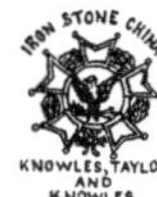

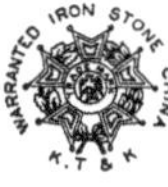

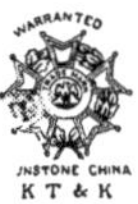

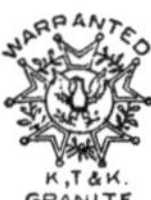


Eagle and monogram mark, on semi-porcelain.
Variation of same.
Another variation of same.
Crescent and Star mark, used on "Lotus" ware.
Variation of same.
Used on white porcelain.
Eagle mark used on various wares.

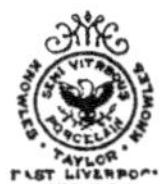

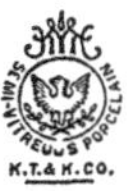

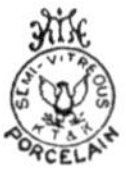

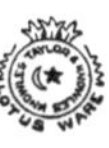

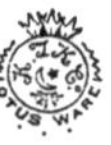

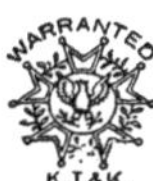


The following marks have been used by The Knowles, Taylor & Knowles Co. on table and toilet services, to indicate the shapes and decorations or patterns:

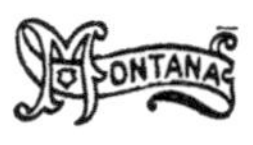

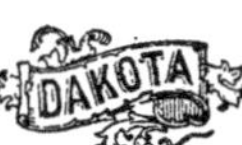

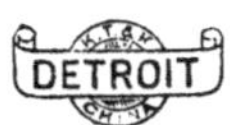

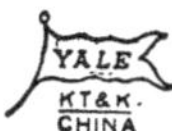

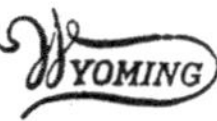

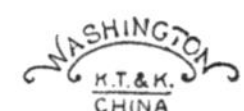

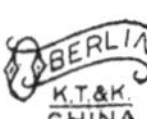

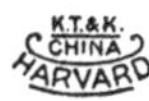


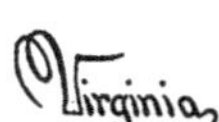

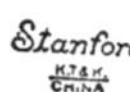

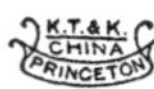

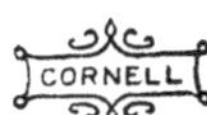

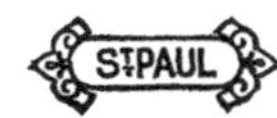


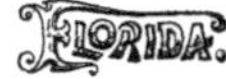

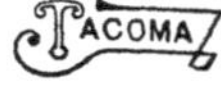

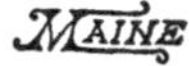

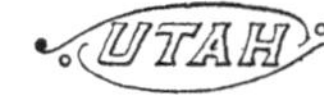

## THE D. E. McNICOL POTTERY CO., EAST LIVERPOOL, OHIO.

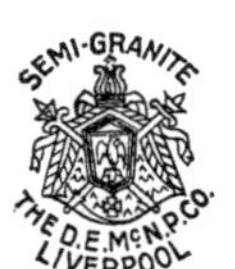


The Novelty Pottery Works, operated by the McNicol Pottery Co., were erected in 1863 by Mr. John Goodwin. The present products are C. C. ware and white granite.

---

## THE C. C. THOMPSON POTTERY CO., EAST LIVERPOOL, OHIO.

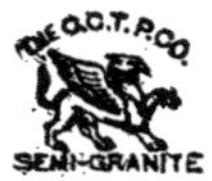


SYDNEY.

LELAND.

OREGON.

Messrs. C. C. Thompson & Co. established a pottery in East Liverpool, Ohio, in 1868. They made a display of pottery at the Centennial in 1876. In 1889 the style was changed to the C. C. Thompson Pottery Co. The products are C. C. and decorated ware, Rockingham and yellow ware.

The mark on their semi-granite ware is a winged lion.

Their toilet services are designated by the names "Sydney," "Leland," "Oregon," etc.

Dinner ware patterns are marked "Melrose," "Drexel," etc.

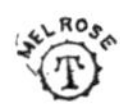


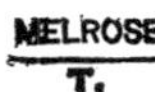


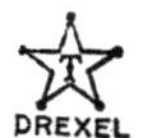


---

## THE HOMER LAUGHLIN CHINA CO., EAST LIVERPOOL, OHIO.

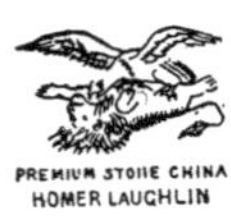


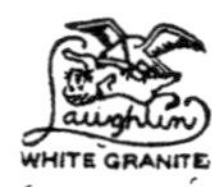


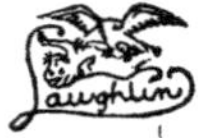


In 1874, Homer and Shakespeare Laughlin established a pottery at East Liverpool, Ohio, under the firm name of Laughlin Bros. From 1879 until 1897 the first named carried on the business alone, and in the latter year the style became the Homer Laughlin China Co. The products of this factory have been mainly white granite, although in later years semi-vitreous china and higher grade wares have been manufactured to some extent. The marks used at this establishment on white granite represent the supremacy of the American Eagle over the British Lion.

The same device is employed in connection with a ring on semi-vitreous china toilet and table services, the name of the pattern being printed beneath, such as "Colonial," "Golden Gate," "An American Beauty."

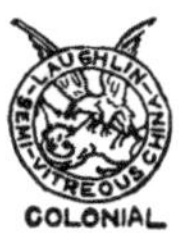

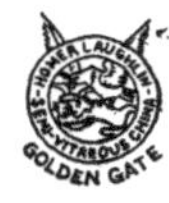

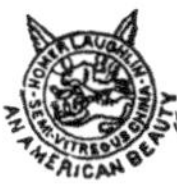


A horseshoe and crossed swords compose the mark that has been used on a line of Laughlin china.

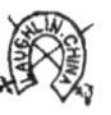

Hotel ware is marked with a monogram, and with a circular stamp.

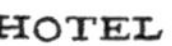

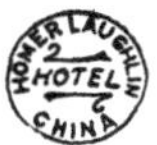


---

## THE POTTERS' CO-OPERATIVE CO., EAST LIVERPOOL, OHIO.

The Dresden works of the Potters' Co-operative Co., of East Liverpool, Ohio, have been in existence since 1876, having been established by Messrs. Brunt, Bloor, Martin & Co. This firm made an exhibit at the Centennial Exposition. Their products are white granite and decorated table and toilet wares, vitreous and hotel china. The following are ware marks:

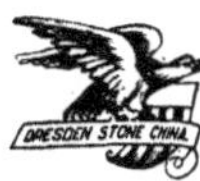

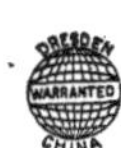

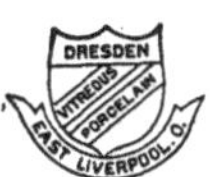

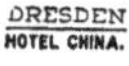

The patterns or shapes are indicated by the marks beneath:

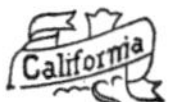


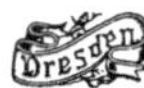


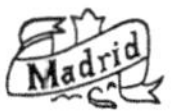


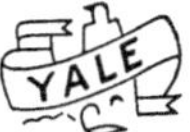


The mark of this company, now used on white granite ware, is a wreath, enclosing the name "Dresden."

The same mark is placed on semi-porcelain.

For hotel china the mark is now *impressed,* in type.

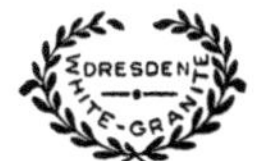


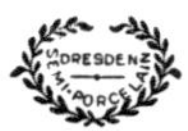


**DRESDEN**
**HOTEL CHINA**
**WARRANTED**

---

## CARTWRIGHT BROTHERS, EAST LIVERPOOL, OHIO.

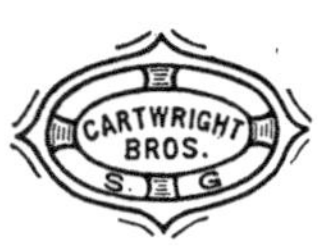


The Industrial Pottery Works are operated by Messrs. Cartwright Brothers. They manufacture C. C. ware, semi-granite, and ivory decorated ware. The mark on their general line is an ellipse enclosing the firm name.

On certain patterns and shapes the marks "Texas," "Avalon," "Brooklyn" and "Elsmere" are placed. The latter appears on dinner ware, the others on toilet sets.

TEXAS. **Avalon** *Brooklyn* *Elsmere*

## THE GLOBE POTTERY CO., EAST LIVERPOOL, OHIO.

The Globe Pottery Co., incorporated in 1888, began making common wares about 1881, under the firm name of Frederick, Shenkle, Allen & Co. The products at present are semi-porcelain toilet and table wares, plain and decorated.

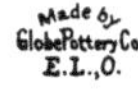


The marks are as follows:

A star on the "Sirius" pattern of toilet ware, in 1896.

A globe on the "Progress" and "Festoon" patterns of dinner ware, in same year.

On specialties, the name of the company, in 1897.

A shell on the "Nautilus" pattern of toilet ware, in 1898.

A globe, surmounted by a crown, on the "Regal" pattern of dinner ware, in 1901.

On hotel china, the initials of the company (see also The East Liverpool Potteries Co.).

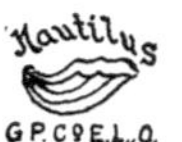


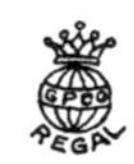


HOTEL
G.P.CO.

## THE WALLACE & CHETWYND POTTERY CO., EAST LIVERPOOL, OHIO.

This company manufactures semi-vitreous opaque china. The mark is a stag's head (see also The East Liverpool Potteries Co.).

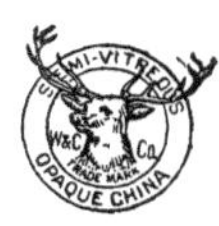


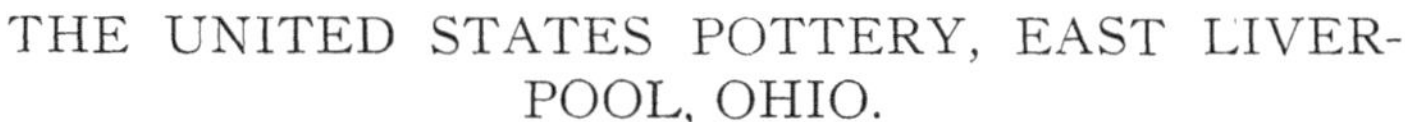

## THE UNITED STATES POTTERY, EAST LIVERPOOL, OHIO.

On their "Raleigh," "Champion" and "Admiral" patterns, the names are marked in written characters (see also The East Liverpool Potteries Co.).

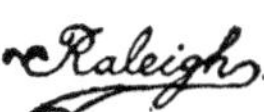


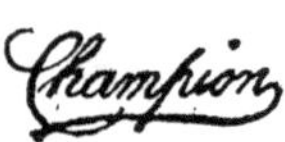


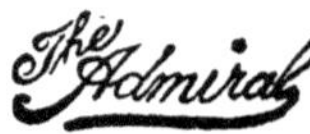

## THE EAST LIVERPOOL POTTERY CO.

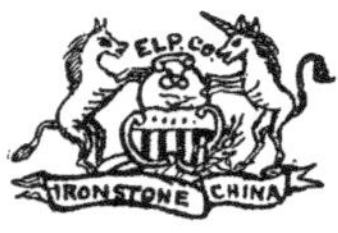


This company, located in East Liverpool, Ohio, manufactures "Waco" china and decorated wares, principally in white granite body. The first mark used was a modification of the British Coat of Arms, which is found on souvenir china made for the Presidential campaign of 1896.

Later marks contained the name "Waco China," in printed letters, and in combination with the company's monogram.

WACO CHINA.

E.L.P.CO.
WACO CHINA

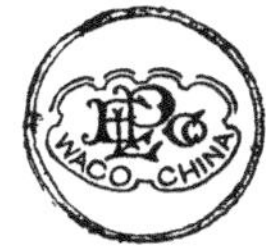


D. of R.
174.

On china made for the order of the Daughters of Rebecca the subjoined mark was placed (see also The East Liverpool Potteries Co.).

---

## THE GEORGE C. MURPHY POTTERY CO., EAST LIVERPOOL, OHIO.

This company succeeded George C. Murphy & Co. The products are semi-porcelain and decorated ware. The marks are here shown (see also The East Liverpool Potteries Co.).

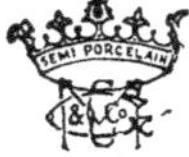


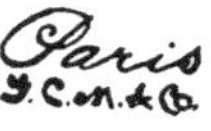


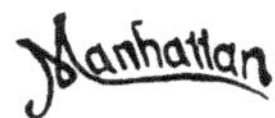


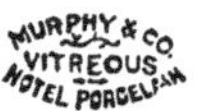

## THE EAST END POTTERY, EAST LIVERPOOL, OHIO.

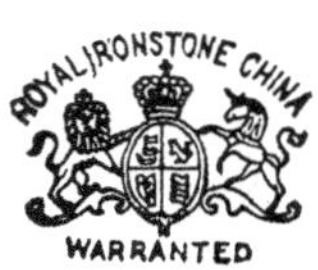


The products of this pottery are white granite, porcelain and decorated wares. The marks are as follows (see also The East Liverpool Potteries Co.).

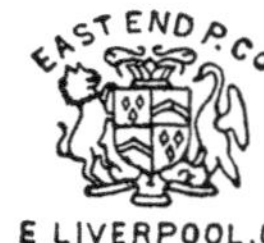

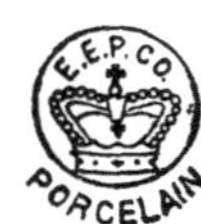

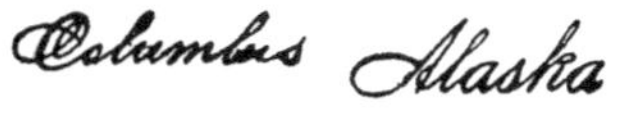

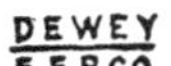


---

## THE EAST LIVERPOOL POTTERIES CO.

This consolidated company now owns and operates the plants of the Globe Pottery, The Wallace & Chetwynd Pottery, The United States Pottery, The East Liverpool Pottery, The George C. Murphy Pottery, and The East End Pottery, all of East Liverpool, Ohio. On all wares produced by these potteries, under the present combination, a uniform mark, the shield of the United States, is printed.

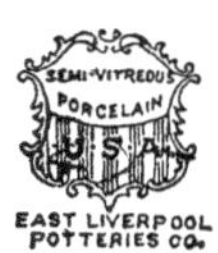


---

## THE UNION POTTERIES CO., EAST LIVERPOOL, OHIO.

The Union Potteries Co., of East Liverpool, Ohio, and Pittsburgh, Pa., uses for a mark a monogram on "Corinne" china.

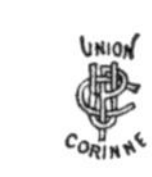


On general ware a wreath was formerly used, enclosing the words "Union China."

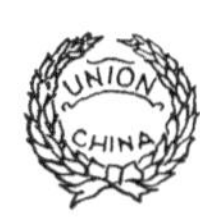


Other marks are an eagle, on "Corinne" china, and a United States flag, on the "Sigsbee" pattern.

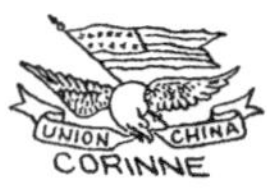

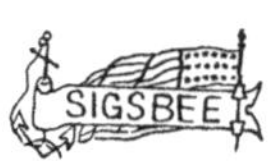

## THE BURFORD BROS. POTTERY CO., EAST LIVERPOOL, OHIO.

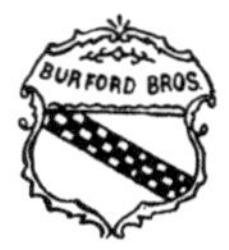


HOTEL

The Burford Bros. Pottery Co. manufactures semi-porcelain ware, plain white and decorated. Various marks have been used by this company.

On their general ware, a shield.

On hotel ware, the word "Hotel."

On porcelain and china bodies:

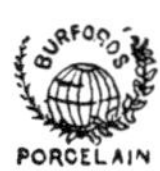

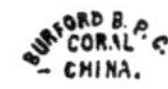


On various shapes and patterns of dinner and toilet wares:

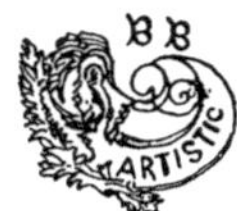


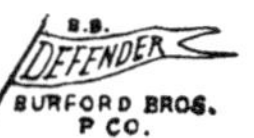


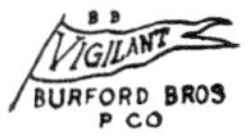


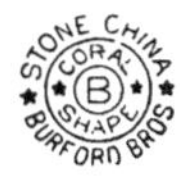


BURFORD BROS.
BEAUTY

Burford Bros
CHAMPION

ELECTRIC

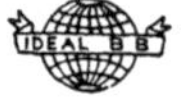


---

## THE TAYLOR, SMITH & TAYLOR CO., EAST LIVERPOOL, OHIO.

TAYLOR
LEE & SMITH CO
GRANITE

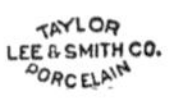


The Taylor, Lee & Smith Co., incorporated in 1899, was the predecessor of the present Taylor, Smith & Taylor Co. The principal product is semi-vitreous porcelain. Subjoined are the marks of the original company, for semi-porcelain and white granite. The marks in use by the present company, for the same wares, are also here shown. The new company began operations on October 1, 1901.

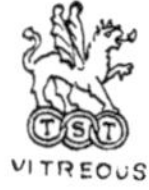

## THE WEST END POTTERY CO., EAST LIVERPOOL, OHIO.

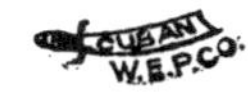


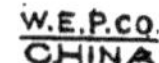


The West End Pottery Co. was organized in 1893, having succeeded Messrs. Burgess & Co. The products are ironstone china and fine decorated ware.

---

## THE SEVRES CHINA CO., EAST LIVERPOOL, OHIO.

This company began business in July, 1900. The mark is a spear head of conventionalized *fleur-de-lis,* adopted from a mark used at the Sevres factory in France about 1830. The regular ware is stamped "Sevres."

On dinner ware is placed the name "Geneva."

Toilet ware is marked "Berlin" and "Melton."

The mark for Hotel China is the name, beneath the word "Sevres."

BERLIN

SÈVRES
HOTEL CHINA

---

## THE EDWIN M. KNOWLES CHINA CO., EAST LIVERPOOL, OHIO.

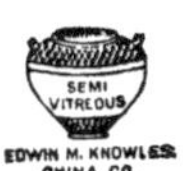


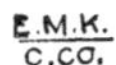


The Edwin M. Knowles China Co. began putting ware on the market in March, 1901. The mark for semi-porcelain is the figure of a vase. That for white granite consists of the initials of the company.

## THE BROCKMANN POTTERY CO., CINCINNATI, OHIO.

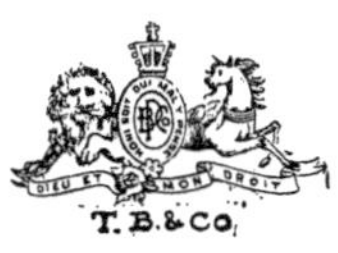


Messrs. Tempest, Brockmann & Co. established a pottery in Cincinnati, Ohio, in 1862. In 1881, the name was changed to the Tempest, Brockmann & Sampson Pottery Co., and in 1887 The Brockmann Pottery Co. was organized by Mr. C. E. Brockmann. The present products are cream-colored and white granite wares. The earliest mark of this establishment was the English lion and unicorn with the initials T. B. & Co. beneath. Since 1887 the same mark has been employed for C. C. ware, with the letters B. P. Co. On white granite the same device is used with the addition of the words "Warranted Best Ironstone China."

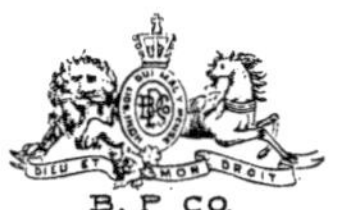


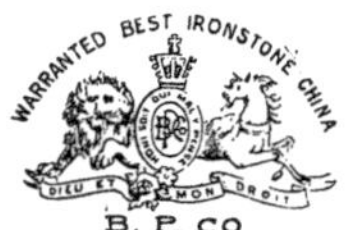


---

## THE ROOKWOOD POTTERY CO., CINCINNATI, OHIO.

The history and achievements of the Rookwood Pottery, Cincinnati, Ohio, are so familiar to every one that it is not considered necessary to review them here. Established in the year 1879 it has steadily forged ahead, under the management of Mr. William W. Taylor, the efficient president of the company, until it now stands in the front rank of American art potteries. Rookwood was the originator of that class of pottery, now so extensively imitated, in which the decorations are painted beneath a brilliant glaze on tinted and blended grounds. The work in every department is thoroughly systematized, and the history of every piece is stamped or painted upon it in a series of marks, which form a portion of the records of the factory.

No pottery in the United States has been so prolific in marks as Rookwood, there being upwards of 130 different devices found stamped upon the wares, exclusive of the numerous record numbers, letters and date symbols. These marks are of five kinds:

1. Factory Marks.
2. Clay or Body Marks.
3. Size Marks.
4. Esoteric or Process Marks.
5. Decorators' Marks.

*Factory Marks.*

The factory marks used at different periods are of twelve varieties. The most common marks prior to 1882 were the name of the pottery and the date of manufacture, which were painted or incised on the base of each piece by the decorator.

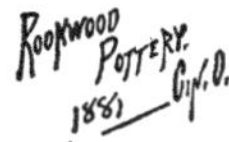

A variation of this consisted of the initials of the pottery and of the founder, R. P. C. O. M. L. N. (Rookwood Pottery, Cincinnati, Ohio, Maria Longworth Nichols).

R.P.C.O.M.L.N.

Previous to 1883 an anchor was stamped in the ware or placed upon it in relief, occasionally in connection with a date. This mark is one of the rarest.

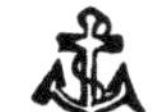

In 1882 a special mark was used on a trade piece—a large beer tankard—made for the Cincinnati Cooperage Co. The letters were *impressed* in a raised ribbon.

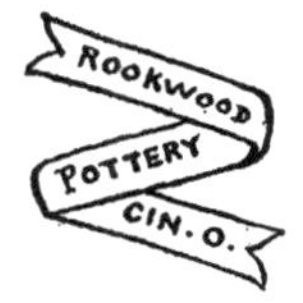


From 1880 to 1882 a design prepared by Mr. H. F. Farny was *printed* in black beneath the glaze. It represents a pottery kiln and two rooks.

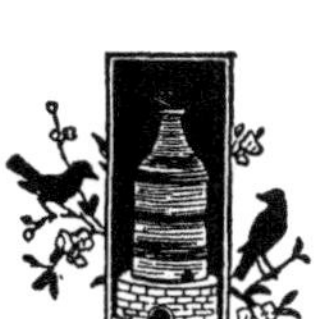

In 1883 a small kiln mark was *impressed* in the ware.

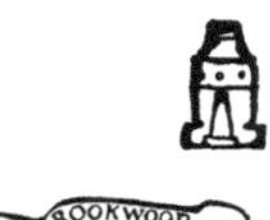

About this period the name of the pottery was stamped on some pieces.

CIN ROOKWOOD POTTERY

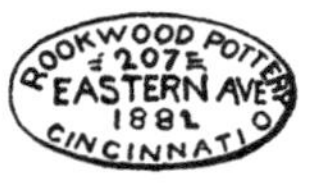


An oval mark, bearing the name and address of the factory and a date, was also used for a short time.

MLS
1897

Mrs. Maria Longworth Storer (Mrs. Bellamy Storer), the founder, has continued her experiments since the factory passed into the hands of the Rookwood Pottery Co., and on many of her recent pieces will be found her initials, which are scratched in the clay, or painted on the surface, frequently accompanied by a date.

ROOKWOOD
1882

The regular mark adopted in 1882 was the word Rookwood and the date, *impressed*. This was continued until 1886, the date being changed each year.

RP

The monogram mark, consisting of the letters R. P., was first adopted in 1886.

RP

In 1887 a flame point was placed above the monogram, and one point has been added each year since. The mark for 1900, therefore, possesses fourteen points.

In 1901 the same mark was used with the addition of a Roman numeral below, to indicate the first year of the new century.

*Clay Marks.*

The clay or body marks consist of six different letters, G. O. R. S. W. and Y., indicating Ginger color, Olive, Red, Sage Green, White, or Yellow, as the case may be:

**G O R S W Y**

*Size Marks.*

The sizes of vases are marked by the letters A to F, inclusive. In connection with these are various numbers, which indicate the shapes and designs. These are entered on the records of the factory.

*Process Marks.*

Esoteric or process marks are occasionally *impressed* on pieces of Rookwood ware, often accompanied by varying record numbers. As these characters only occur on experimental pieces, they are seldom found on examples which leave the factory, and their significance is never divulged. For the benefit of those who may come across such marks, however, they are here shown:

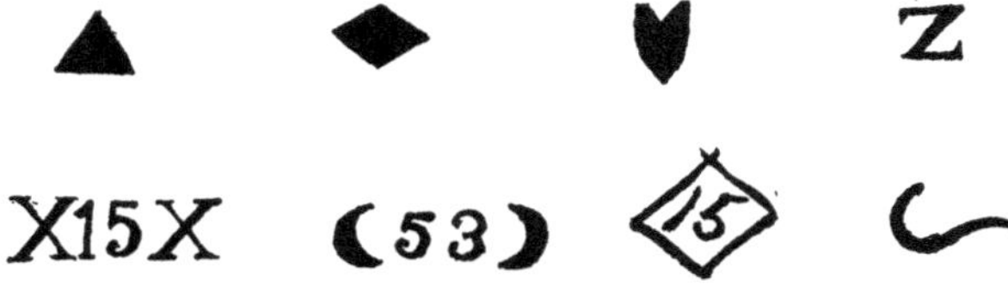


*Decorators' Marks.*

It is customary at the Rookwood Pottery for the decorators to cut their initials or monograms on the bottoms of pieces painted by them. Among the decorators are many who stand high in their profession, not only as underglaze painters, but as artists in water colors and oil. Possessors of beautifully executed designs in Rookwood will be interested in learning the names of the painters. These pieces will increase in value as the years go by. The following is believed to be a complete presentation of the marks of all regular decorators who have been connected with the pottery since its beginning:

A.R.V.—Albert R. Valentien.
A.H.—Albert Humphreys.
A.B.—Alfred Brennan.
A.M.B.—Miss A. M. Bookprinter (2 marks).
A.M.V.—Mrs. Anna M. Valentien.
A.B.S.—Miss Amelia B. Sprague (4 marks).
A.V.B.—Artus Van Briggle (2 marks).
A.G.—Arthur Goetting.
A.D.S.—Miss Adeliza D. Sehon.

B.—Bruce Horsfall.
C.N.—Miss Clara Chipman Newton (2 marks).
M.M.—Miss Marianne Mitchell.
C.S.—Miss Carrie Steinle (3 marks).
C.A.B.—Miss Constance A. Baker.
C.J.D.—Charles John Dibowski.
C.C.—Miss Cora Crofton.
C.S.—Charles Schmidt (2 marks).
C.C.L.—Miss Clara C. Lindeman.
D.C.—Daniel Cook.
E.P.C.—Edward P. Cranch (2 marks).
E.D.F.—Miss Emma D. Foertmeyer.
E.A.—Edward Abel.
E.B.I.C.—Miss E. Bertha I. Cranch.
E.D.—E. D. Diers.
E.T.H.—E. T. Hurley.
C.F.B.—Miss Caroline Bonsall.
E.R.F.—Miss Edith R. Felten.
E.W.B.—Miss Elizabeth W. Brain.
E.C.L.—Miss Eliza C. Lawrence.
F.A.—Miss Fannie Auckland.
F.V.—F. W. Vreeland.
H.W.—Miss Harriet Wenderoth.
H.H.—Miss Hattie Horton.
H.E.W.—Miss Harriet E. Willcox.
H.R.S.—Miss Harriet R. Strafer.
H.A.—Howard Altman.
I.B.—Miss Irene Bishop.
J.D.W.—J. Dee Wareham (3 marks).
K.C.M.—Miss Kate C. Matchette.
K., F.D.K.—Mrs. F. D. Koehler.
G.H.—Miss Grace M. Hall.
K.H.—Miss Katharine Hickman.
L.A.F.—Miss Laura A. Fry (2 marks).
L.N.L.—Miss Lizzie N. Lingenfelter.
L.A.—Miss Leonore Asbury.
L.V.B.—Miss Leona Van Briggle.
L.E.L.—Miss Laura E. Lindeman (2 marks).
M.L.S.—Mrs. Maria Longworth Storer.
M.R.—Martin Rettig.

M.A.D.—Matt A. Daly.
M.T., M.A.T.—Miss Mary L. Taylor (2 marks).
M.L.P.—Miss Mary L. Perkins (3 marks).
M.N.—Miss Mary Nourse.
L.E.H.—Miss Lena E. Hanscom.
M.R.—Miss Marie Rauchfuss.
M.F.—Miss Mattie Foglesong.
M.H.S.—Miss Marion H. Smalley.
N.J.H.—N. J. Hirschfeld.
O.G.R.—Miss O. Geneva Reed. (Mrs. Geneva Reed Pinney.)
P.P.—Miss Pauline Peters.
F.R.—Fred Rothenbusch.
R.F.—Miss Rose Fechheimer (2 marks).
H.P.S.—Miss H. Pabodie Stuntz.
S.M.—Miss Sadie Markland.
S.E.C.—Miss Sallie Coyne (2 marks).
S.L.—Sturgis Lawrence.
S.S.—Miss Sara Sax (3 marks).
J.S.—Miss Jeannette Swing.
S.T.—Miss Sallie Toohey (3 marks).
T.O.M.—Tom Lunt.
V.B.D.—Miss Virginia B. Demarest (2 marks).
W.H.B.—W. H. Breuer (2 marks).
W.P.McD.—W. P. McDonald (4 marks).
W.K.—William Klemm.
G.Y.—Miss Grace Young.
J.E.Z.—Miss Josephine E. Zettel (2 marks).

Mark of Kataro Shirayamadani, a Japanese artist (see accompanying table).

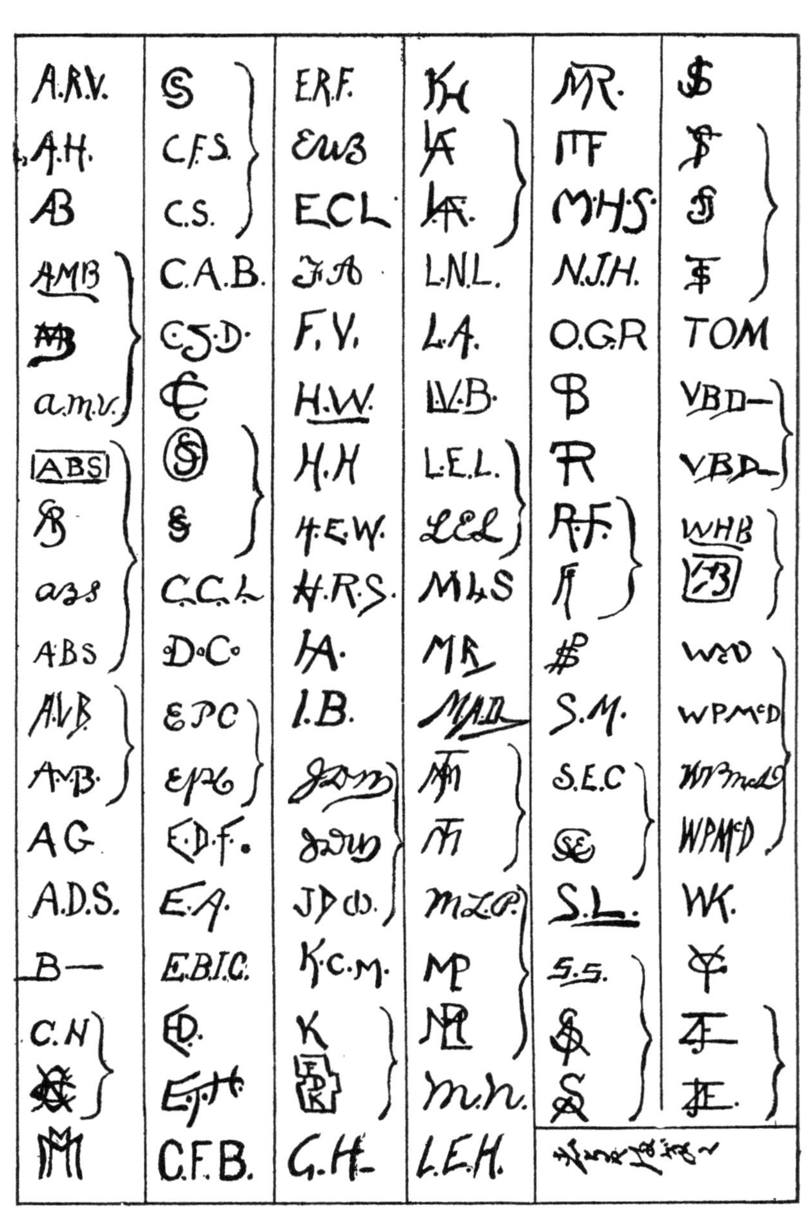

Private Marks of Rookwood Decorators.

## THE CINCINNATI ART POTTERY CO.

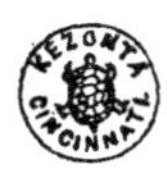


The Cincinnati Art Pottery Co., with Frank Huntington as president, commenced operations in Cincinnati, Ohio, in 1879. A variety of artistic wares was produced, such as underglaze faience, barbotine ware, "Hungarian," "Portland Blue" and "Ivory-Colored Faience." Three distinguishing marks were employed, the first one being the figure of a turtle. About 1886 the Indian name for turtle, "Kezonta," was added, being *printed* on the finer grades of ware in *red*. On the plainer wares, such as blue glazed and white pottery, furnished in artistic shapes for decorators, the word "Kezonta" was *impressed*.

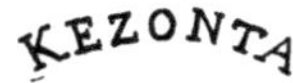


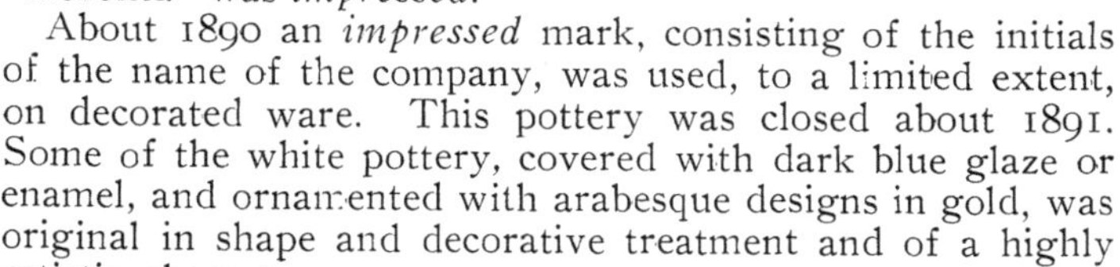

About 1890 an *impressed* mark, consisting of the initials of the name of the company, was used, to a limited extent, on decorated ware. This pottery was closed about 1891. Some of the white pottery, covered with dark blue glaze or enamel, and ornamented with arabesque designs in gold, was original in shape and decorative treatment and of a highly artistic character.

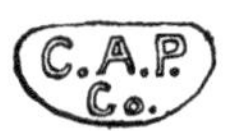


## MATT MORGAN ART POTTERY COMPANY, CINCINNATI, OHIO.

About the year 1883 an art pottery was established in Cincinnati, Ohio, by Matt Morgan, an English artist, who had a few years before been brought to this country by the publisher of a New York periodical.

In Cincinnati he afterwards met George Ligowsky, the inventor of clay pigeons, and as Morgan had formerly obtained some knowledge of pottery making in Spain he induced Ligowsky to make some trials with certain clays and furnished some pieces of Spanish-Moresque ware as suggestions toward the development of an art product. This was the beginning of the Matt Morgan Pottery, which was later turned into a stock company.

This venture was at first quite promising. The wares produced were original in design and treatment. Slip-decorated pottery in the Limoges underglaze style was developed along original lines. Moresque pottery was also produced in rich colorings and lustres, artistically modeled and profusely gilded. Some of the pieces were covered with a brilliant glaze, while others possessed a matt finish. Competent decorators, such as Matt A. Daly and other now prominent painters, worked enthusiastically, and the shapes were principally designed and modeled by Herman C. Mueller in conjunction with Mr. Morgan.

The cause of the failure of the company after about a year was caused by the effort of the stockholders to place the business on a commercial basis, at the expense of the artistic element. After the company failed, the molds, models and remaining stock of ware were practically thrown away. Very few art potteries in this country started under as favorable circumstances as did the Matt Morgan pottery, and some of the pieces which were turned out reveal a high order of artistic merit, while many of the best examples are now owned by art connoisseurs in Cincinnati and other places.

MATT MORGAN
ART POTTERY CO.

Mr. Morgan closed his career as art director of a large lithographic establishment. He died a few years ago.

MATT MORGAN
-CIN. O-
ART POTTERY CO.

The mark used on some of the pieces was the title of the company, *impressed,* sometimes containing the abbreviated name of the city in the centre and sometimes without.

N.J.H.

The initials of the decorators were also scratched in the clay. One of these was Mr. N. J. Hirschfeld.

Mr. Mueller, who is now connected with The National Tile Co., of Morrisville, Pa., has furnished the above information from his personal knowledge.

---

## AVON POTTERY, CINCINNATI, OHIO.

The Avon Pottery was founded in January, 1886, and was in existence for a period of about a year and a half to two years. One variety of ware produced here was made of yellow clay, decorated in colored slips and modeled or etched in part. This was treated in a "smear" or dull glaze finish. Another variety was made of white clay, decorated with atomized colors and painted designs on the biscuit and covered with a brilliant transparent glaze. The effect of the atomized coloring was a gradual shading of the ground from light to darker tints, in pink, olive, violet, blue, brown, etc. All of the pieces were thrown on the wheel, while some were furnished with modeled handles. In the Pennsylvania Museum collection are several small vases of this character, including two with green tinted ground and covers, and handles in the form of elephants' heads. In the collection of Dr. Marcus Benjamin, of Washington, D. C., is a mug-shaped cup of graceful shape with a tinted ground shading from white to dark pink, and a modeled ram's horn handle. Some of the pieces made at this pottery were marked with the name AVON.

AVON

---

## MISS M. LOUISE McLAUGHLIN, CINCINNATI, OHIO.

Miss M. Louise McLaughlin, who has been identified with the pottery movement in Cincinnati since the Centennial in 1876, has, during the past five years, been experimenting in porcelain bodies, and has now perfected several new bodies which she will hereafter produce at a little pottery erected on the grounds adjoining her residence. The marks she is using are her monogram, and the name "Losanti," derived from the early name of the city, Losantiville. These are usually *impressed* in the paste, but occasionally *painted* in blue.

Losanti

---

## THE WELLSVILLE CHINA CO., WELLSVILLE, OHIO.

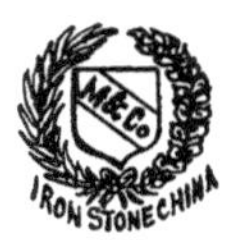


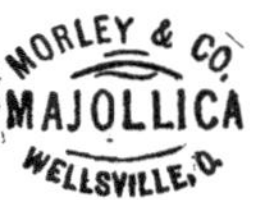


Messrs. Morley & Co. established a pottery in this place in 1879, for the production of white granite and majolica. The marks used on these wares are here shown. For the former, the design consisted of a wreath enclosing a shield bearing the firm's initials. For the latter, the name of the ware with the firm's name and address.

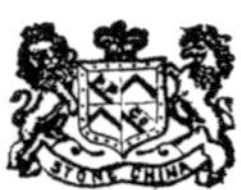


In 1885, the Pioneer Pottery Co. was organized. On white granite the lion and unicorn supporting a shield was used. On their "Imperial China," a garter or strap, enclosing the company's monogram, was employed, and on porcelain a circular stamp bearing the initials of the works.

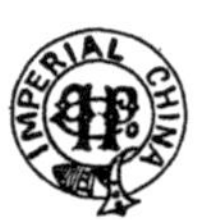


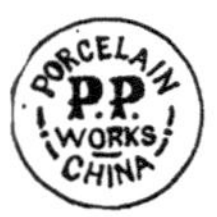


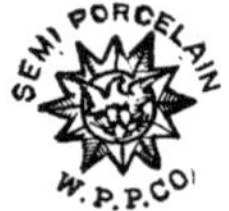


In 1896, a new company was formed under the name of the Wellsville Pioneer Pottery Co. The principal product was semi-porcelain. Two marks were used, a star with eagle in the centre, and the initials of the company in type.

W.P.P.Co.
SEMI-PORCELAIN

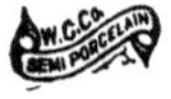


Later, these works, having changed hands, were operated by the Wellsville China Co., semi-porcelain continuing to be made under the new management.

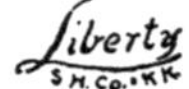


The "Liberty" mark was used at one time on a special order of goods for a customer.

## J. H. BAUM, WELLSVILLE, OHIO.

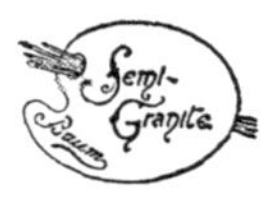


J. H. Baum manufactured semi-granite ware for some time previous to 1897, at which date the factory was closed.

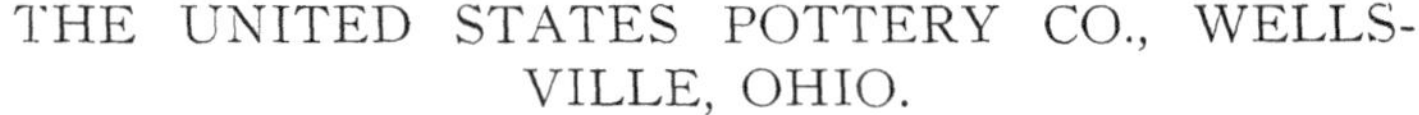

## THE UNITED STATES POTTERY CO., WELLSVILLE, OHIO.

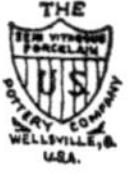


This company began operations in 1899. They manufacture a high grade of semi-vitreous porcelain. The mark is the shield of the United States.

## THE STEUBENVILLE POTTERY CO., STEUBENVILLE, OHIO.

The Steubenville Pottery Co. was formed in November of 1879, for the purpose of manufacturing white granite and other wares. About ten years after the company commenced operations a new, semi-vitreous, opaque body, of a rich cream color and unusually light weight, was introduced under the name of "Canton china," which has since formed an important specialty of the factory. At present the products consist of semi-vitreous and porcelain, granite and decorated wares.

The marks used to indicate particular shapes in toilet and dinner services are as follows:

"Beula," the map of the State of Ohio.

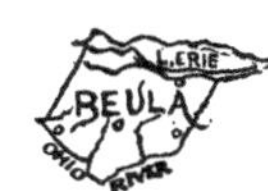


"Florence," a pinned label.

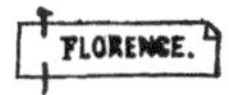


"Belle," an ornamented label.

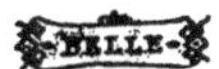

"Vesta," a suspended label.

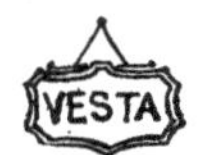


"Clio," the name in fancy lettering.

"Don," a shield in a ring.

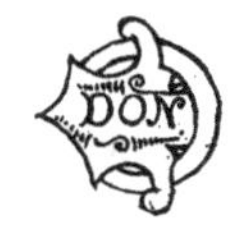


"Day," a painter's palette. Mr. Day was formerly secretary of the company.

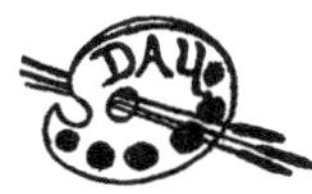


The above pattern marks were in use between 1890 and 1895.

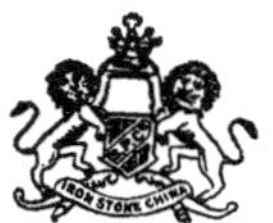


The marks used on the general lines of white granite and "Canton" china are,—

Two lions supporting a shield, on white granite.

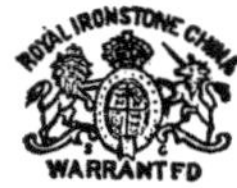


The British Arms, on the same.

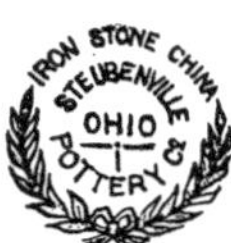


A wreath enclosing the company's name, also on white granite.

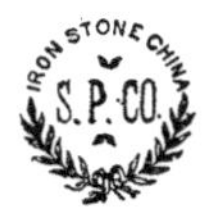


A modification of same mark.

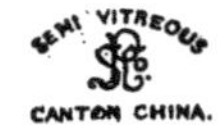


The monogram of the company, on semi-vitreous "Canton" china.

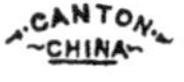


The name of the ware on "Canton" china.

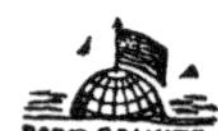


A submerged globe and U. S. flag, on porcelain granite.

---

## THE LONHUDA POTTERY.

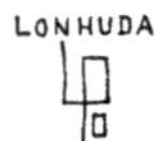


The Lonhuda Pottery was established at Steubenville, Ohio, in 1892. The name was derived from the first syllables of the names of the projectors, Messrs. Long, Hunter and Day. The pottery, after a few years, was moved to Zanesville, Ohio. The products were underglaze slip-painted wares with shaded and blended grounds. The mark first employed was the monogram of the company, in conventionalized style.

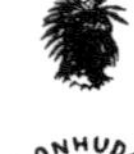

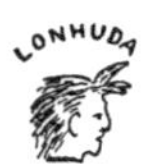


In 1893, a new mark was adopted, consisting of an Indian's head. This was used on shapes adapted from aboriginal American pottery forms. A profile head was used later.

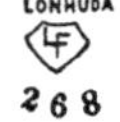


In 1896, the shield mark was substituted. All of these were *impressed* in the clay.

Other marks which occur on Lonhuda pottery are the initials and monograms of the decorators, as follows:

Miss Laura A. Fry.

Miss Sarah R. McLaughlin.

Miss Helen M. Harper.

Mr. W. A. Long.

Miss Jessie R. Spaulding.

The numbers impressed on Lonhuda pieces relate to the forms.

At a later date Dr. W. A. Long, one of the original members of the firm, went to Denver, Col., where he organized a new company. Lonhuda ware is now being made there (see the Denver China and Pottery Co.).

---

## S. A. WELLER, ZANESVILLE, OHIO.

Eosian
WELLER

Aurelian
WELLER

LOUWELSA
WELLER

DICKENS WARE
WELLER

TURADA
WELLER

SICARDO
WELLER.

S. A. Weller produces several varieties of art potteries in underglaze decorations. They are known as "Eosian," "Aurelian," "Louwelsa" (a word formed by the combination of the names of the manufacturer, and his daughter Louise), "Auroral," "Dickens" and "Turada" wares. "Dickens" ware is entirely different from the others, having a matt finish. The marks are the names of these wares.

In 1901, Mr. J. Sicard, formerly connected with the pottery of Clement Massier of Golfe Juan, France, came to the United States and resumed his experiments in metallic lustre work at the pottery of Mr. S. A. Weller, Zanesville, Ohio. He has now perfected an art ware which has been named Sicardo-Weller ware. The decoration consists of floral and other devices in metallic lustres on an iridescent ground of different tints, the effect being novel and highly artistic.

The following marks of decorators are found on art ware produced at this pottery:

Virginia Adams.

Elizabeth Ayers.

Lizabeth Blake.

Levi J. Burgess.

Anna Dautherty.

Anthony Dunlavy.

Frank Ferrell.

Mary Gillie.

Albert Haubrich.

Madge Hurst.

Josephine Imlay.

Karl Kappes.

S. Reid McLaughlin.

Hattie Mitchell.

Lillie Mitchell.

Minnie Mitchell.

Gordon Mull.

Edwin Pickens.

Hester W. Pillsbury.

Eugene Roberts.

Tot Steele.

C. Minnie Terry.

Helen B. Windle.

---

## THE J. B. OWENS POTTERY CO., ZANESVILLE, OHIO.

This company manufactures art vases, lamps, jardinières, pedestals and specialties with underglaze decorations, which are painted by competent artists. A considerable corps of decorators is employed, who place their names or initials on their work. Possessors of art wares are always interested in knowing something about the pieces which come into their possession. For their benefit a list of these painters and their marks is here given:

Estelle Beardsley.

Edith Bell. EB

Fanny Bell. FB

A. F. Best.

Cecilia Bloomer.

Lillian Bloomer. L.B.

Cora Davis. C.D.

W. Denny. WD

Harrie Eberlein.

Hattie Eberlein. HE

Cecil Excel. CE

Charles Gray.

Martha E. Gray. M.G.

Delores Harvey. D.H.

Albert Haubrich. A Haubrich

Roy Hook.

H. Hoskins.

Harry Larzelere.

A. V. Lewis. AL

Cora McCandless.

Carrie McDonald.

Miss Oshe. O

Mary L. Peirce. MP

Harry Robinson.

Hattie M. Ross. HMR.

R. Lillian Shoemaker.

Ida Steele.

Will H. Stemm. WHS

Mary Fauntleroy Stevens.

Mae Timberlake. M.T.

Sarah Timberlake. S.T.

Arthur Williams.

The marks used on several distinct varieties or styles of ware, "Utopian," "Feroza" and "Henri Deux," are shown.

OWENS UTOPIAN    OWENS FEROZA    HENRI DEUX

Sometimes other marks will be found on pieces from this establishment. These are experimental marks, of no significance to the purchaser, but relating to certain records at the factory. The more common of these are here figured. The last one represents a series of such marks in which any letter *plus* a figure or number may be used.

# 1-2    # 3-3-3    X III-III-III    1-2 X    B+II

## THE AMERICAN ENCAUSTIC TILING CO., ZANESVILLE, OHIO.

H.M.

A.E.T. Co.

Embossed tiles made by the American Encaustic Tiling Co., of Zanesville, Ohio, and marked H. M., were modeled by Herman C. Mueller, previous to 1893.

The products of this factory are usually stamped on the back with the initials of the company.

## THE MOSAIC TILE CO., ZANESVILLE, OHIO.

This company was organized by Mr. Herman C. Mueller and Mr. Karl Langenbeck for the manufacture of mosaic tiling. The designs are produced by sifting the different colors of powdered clay through stencils and subjecting the die to great pressure. The effect is that of mosaic work. The mark stamped in the back of the tiles is the monogram of the company.

## THE FRENCH CHINA CO., SEBRING, OHIO.

The French China Co. manufactures table and toilet wares in white granite and semi-porcelain bodies. On "La Francaise" porcelain the accompanying mark is used.

La Francaise Porcelain

On different patterns and shapes the following appear:

The "Lygia" dinner ware.

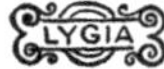


The "Greek" toilet service.

Greek

The "Kenneth" toilet set.

Kenneth

The "Tiger" toilet service.

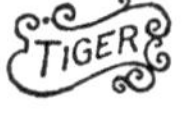


The "Pluto" toilet set.

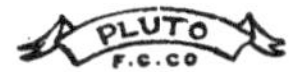


The "Cupid" toilet pattern.

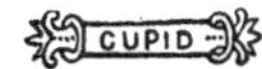


---

## THE SEBRING POTTERY CO., SEBRING, OHIO.

Messrs. Sebring Brothers & Co. established The American Pottery Works at East Liverpool, Ohio, in 1887, for the manufacture of white granite and other decorated wares in dinner and tea services.

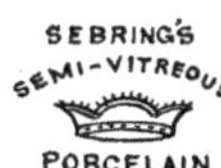


The Sebring Pottery Co. is now making semi-vitreous and porcelain wares at Sebring, Ohio. The marks used on these bodies, and on their "Kokus" china, are here figured.

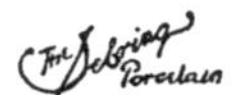


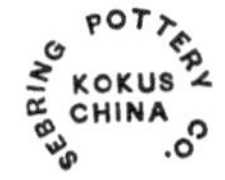

## THE OLIVER CHINA CO., SEBRING, OHIO.

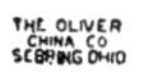


VERUS
PORCELAIN

The Oliver China Co. manufactures "Verus" porcelain, in dinner and toilet sets, jardinières, pedestals and specialties, such as clocks, fancy dishes, fern trays and articles for the wholesale drug trade and hospitals. This pottery has been in operation since October, 1899.

The marks are the name of the company in type, and "Verus Porcelain."

---

## THE EAST PALESTINE POTTERY CO., EAST PALESTINE, OHIO.

The East Palestine Pottery Co. manufactures semi-porcelain, jardinières and specialties, plain and decorated.

The mark is a wreath enclosing the company's monogram, with the name of the pattern beneath, such as "Revere," "Columbia," etc.

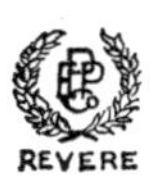


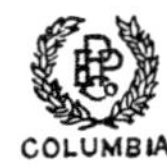


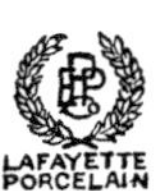


---

## THE OHIO CHINA CO., EAST PALESTINE, OHIO.

O.C.CO
LIMOGES
PORCELAIN

The Ohio China Co. uses as a trade-mark on "Limoges Porcelain" the initials of the company and the name of the ware.

---

## THE CROOKSVILLE CHINA CO., CROOKSVILLE, OHIO.

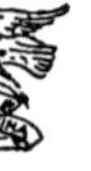

The Crooksville China Co. produces high-grade porcelain, semi-vitreous and decorated toilet and dinner wares. The mark is a dove bearing in its beak a scroll inscribed with the company's name.

## THE AMERICAN CHINA CO., TORONTO, OHIO.

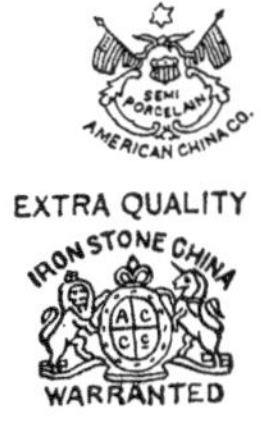


The American China Co. was organized in 1897 for the manufacture of semi-porcelain and white granite wares.

On the former a mark, composed of flags and shield, is used.

The Arms of Great Britain appear on white granite ware.

Toilet-set patterns are marked with the name, as "Biltmore," "Eugenia," etc.

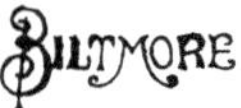


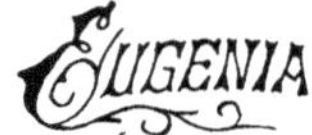


## THE CAMBRIDGE ART POTTERY CO., CAMBRIDGE, OHIO.

This company manufactures faience vases, jardinières, pedestals and clay specialties. The mark is an acorn bearing the monogram of the company. The various patterns and shapes of services are printed beneath, such as "Oakwood," "Cambridge," "Acorn" and "Guernsey."

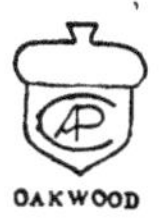


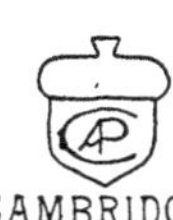


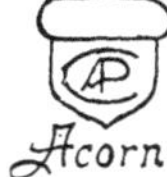


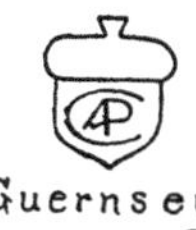


## THE BRADSHAW CHINA CO., NILES, OHIO.

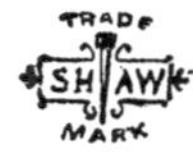


The Bradshaw China Co. produces white granite ware of a superior quality. The decorations are mainly in the decalcomania style.

The mark is a brad piercing the word "shaw."

## THE THOMAS CHINA CO., LISBON, OHIO.

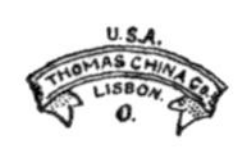


Thomas
China Co.

The Thomas China Co. makes dinner and toilet sets in semi-porcelain. Also hotel wares, jardinières and specialties. The marks are composed of the name of the company.

---

## THE AKRON CHINA CO., AKRON, OHIO.

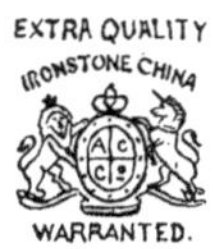


The Akron China Co. manufactures decorated dinner and toilet wares and specialties in white granite and hotel ware. The marks are the British Arms for white granite, and a monogram for "Revere" china.

---

## THE FLORENTINE POTTERY CO., CHILLICOTHE, OHIO.

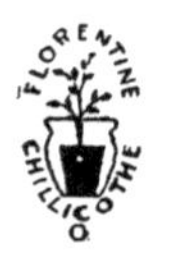


The Florentine Pottery Co. makes a specialty of faience and art ware, such as vases, pedestals, jardinières and umbrella stands. The mark is a flower-pot surrounded by the names of the pottery and the town.

---

## THE BELL POTTERY CO., FINDLAY, OHIO.

THE BELL POTTERY CO
FINDLAY OHIO

BELL CHINA
B. P. Co.
Findlay, Ohio

B P Co
F O

The Bell Pottery Co. produces vitreous translucent china.
The accompanying mark is *impressed* in the heavier ware.
Mark used on hotel china.
Mark *printed* on their china fancy articles, under the glaze.

## ROSEVILLE POTTERY, ZANESVILLE, OHIO.

Among the recent applicants for popular favor is the Roseville Pottery Company of Zanesville, Ohio. The ware produced there is underglaze decorated pottery made from local clays. It is *cast* in molds and ground-tinted by spraying and blending the colors by means of compressed air brushes. The decorations are then painted with slip colors on the damp clay and when thoroughly dry the ware is subjected to its first firing. The glaze is then applied and the pieces are fired a second time. The mark is a circle enclosing a rose and the name "Rozane Ware."

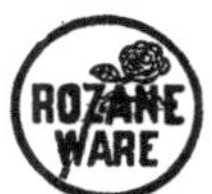


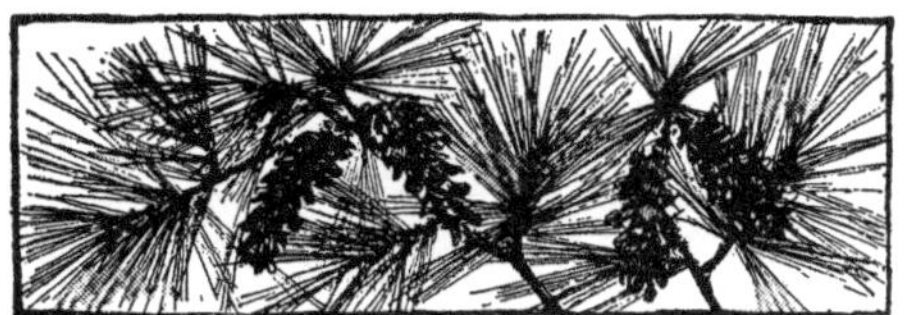

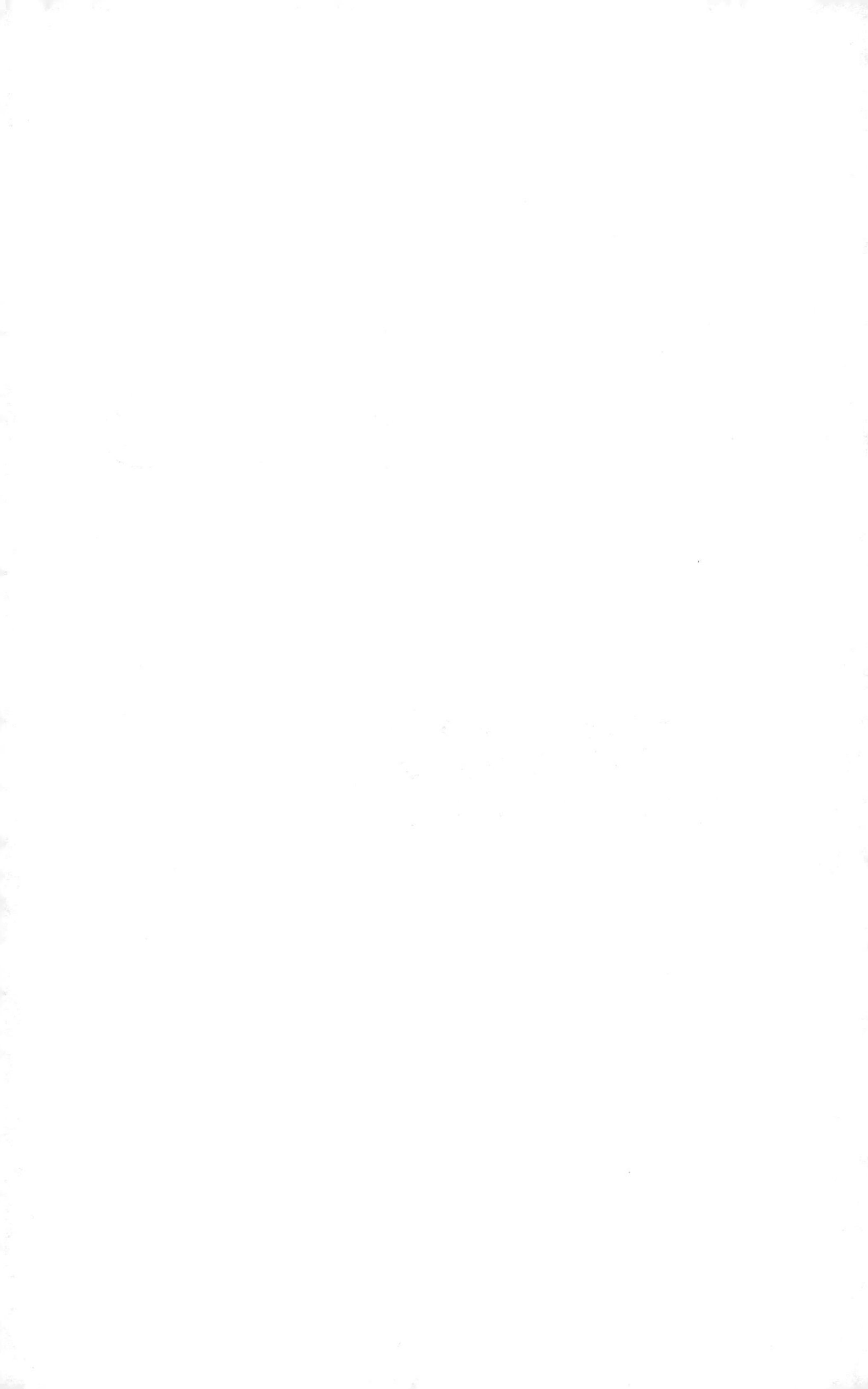

# POTTERIES
# OF THE SOUTHERN STATES

---

# SOUTHERN STATES.

## THE EDWIN BENNETT POTTERY CO., BALTIMORE, MD.

JAMES BENNETT erected a pottery for the manufacture of yellow and Rockingham ware in East Liverpool, Ohio, in 1839. This was the pioneer pottery of what is now the greatest pottery-producing section in the United States. In 1844, Mr. Bennett, with his three brothers, moved the plant to Birmingham, Pittsburg, Pa. The mark used at this time was the name of the firm *"Bennett Bros."*

In 1846, Edwin Bennett withdrew from the firm and went to Baltimore, where he erected a small pottery. Two years later he was joined by his brother, William. The mark used at this period consisted of the firm name and address. The wares produced were stoneware of various colors, Egyptian black ware and a variety of "majolica" that was introduced about 1850. This mark was discontinued about 1856, when William Bennett withdrew.

E. & W. BENNETT
CANTON AVENUE
BALTIMORE MD.

Charles Coxon began modeling for this firm in 1850, and many of their pitcher forms, which were made in brown or Rockingham glaze, were designed and modeled by him. Among these were the Wild Boar pitcher, modeled in 1851; the Rebekah at the Well teapot, in 1852, which, however, was adapted from an earlier model produced by S. Alcock & Co., of Burslem, Staffordshire, the original being a Parian jug with blue ground and raised figure of Rebekah in white; the Hunting jug, with relief figures of hunters on horseback, and stags and hounds on the reverse side; the Stork pitcher, in 1853; a Game jug, Grape-Vine coffee pot, Forrester milk pitcher, Oak Stump vase, and a large water or coffee urn with dolphin handles and relief grape-vine decorations (see illustration 32). Afterwards Mr. Coxon went to Trenton, N. J., and established a pottery there (see Coxon & Co.).

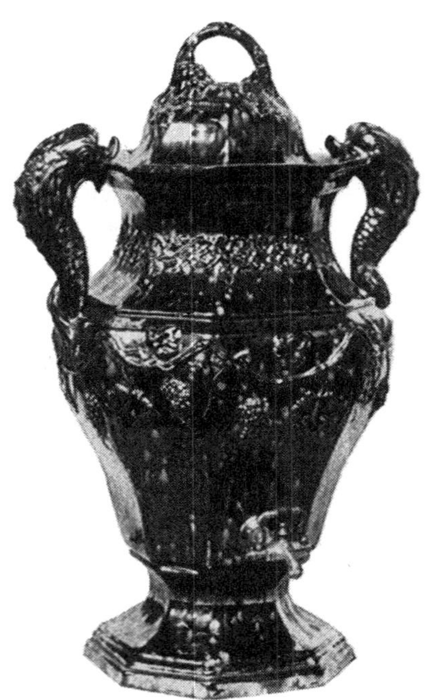

32. Rockingham Coffee Urn.
Modeled by Charles Coxon.
By E. & W. Bennett,
Baltimore, Md., 1853.

For about twenty years no other marks appear to have been employed. In 1875 the Phœnix mark was used on white granite ware.

In 1880, a seven-pointed star, enclosing the initials of the manufacturer, was adopted for stone china.

In 1884, the mark for cream-colored ware was a globe in a circle, surrounded by the word WARRANTED.

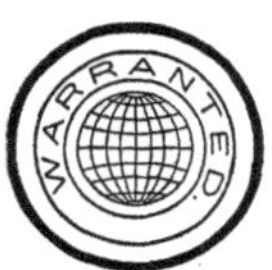


In 1884 and 1885, copyright and patent marks were used on Parian plaques, with relief designs of heads of cattle and other specialties, modeled by Mr. James Priestman. These were among the best things of the kind that had been produced down to that time, and were modeled from life.

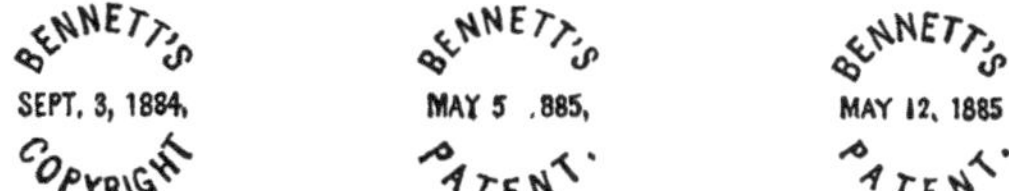


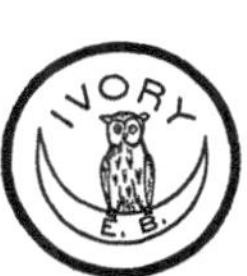


In 1886, the owl mark was used on "Ivory" chamber sets and jugs. In the same year the mark for stone china consisted of a design of two deers supporting a shield. Mr. Bennett had been importuned by the trade to adopt the English mark, which he refused to do, but compromised by using this device, which is, in reality, though perhaps not intended to be, a modification of the Arms of the State of Michigan. An additional mark for stone china or white granite ware was used to some extent in 1886. This was a square enclosing a circle inscribed "Warranted Stone China."

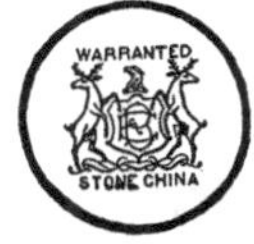


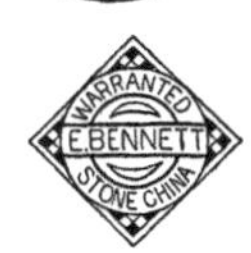


In 1890, when the Edwin Bennett Pottery Co. was organized, the mark adopted was a globe, pierced through the United States by a sword, on the guard of which the initials of the company appear. The motto which forms a part of the mark is "Bona Fama est Melior Zona Aurea." This

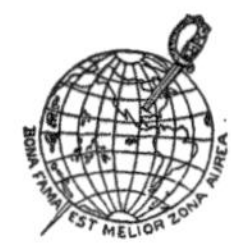

continues to be used on all semi-porcelain wares. Several variations are found on special wares.

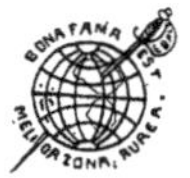

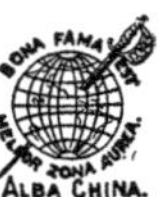


SEMI GRANITE
E.B.P.
Co.

In 1892, the Semi-Granite stamp was placed on cream-colored ware.

In 1896, the Coronet stamp was employed as a mark on an English printed body.

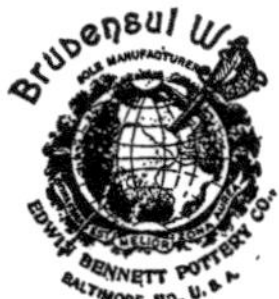


In 1894, the company began the manufacture of their "Brubensul" ware, a highly glazed variety of "majolica." The name was formed by the combination of the first syllables of the names of the firm—Brunt, Bennett and Sullivan. The mark appears as a large paper label attached to the bottoms of jardinières and other pieces.

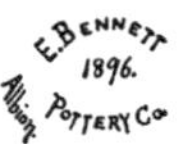


In 1895, the production of slip-painted ware was commenced, which was called "Albion" ware, because slip decorating had been done in England at an early period. This was decorated beneath the glaze and possessed a distinct art value and elements of originality. The mark consisted of the name of the company and of the ware and the date of production.

KB

HB

AB

The foremost decorator of the Albion ware was Miss Kate De Witt Berg, a former pupil of the Pennsylvania Museum and School of Industrial Art, Philadelphia, Pa. Her monogram appears on pieces painted by her, either in printing or writing letters.

Miss Annie Haslam Brinton, also of Philadelphia, was another decorator of Albion ware. Her mark was a monogram of her initials.

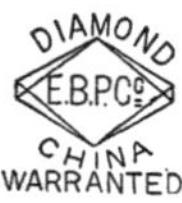


In 1896, the diamond mark was used on a hard grade of china, which was only produced for a short while.

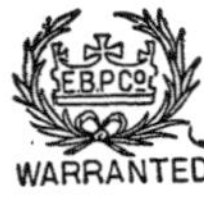


From 1897 to the present time a modification of the earlier coronet stamp has been in use for cream-colored ware.

## THE MARYLAND POTTERY CO., BALTIMORE, MD.

The Maryland Queensware Factory was erected in 1879 by Messrs. Hamill & Bullock. They were succeeded in 1880 by Hamill, Brown & Co. The Maryland Pottery Co. was incorporated in 1888, since which date the plant has been considerably altered and enlarged. Following are the marks of the different owners of the works: On white granite china made for Messrs. D. F. Haynes & Co., of Baltimore, their selling agents and wholesale dealers in crockery, glass, etc. (afterwards proprietors of the Chesapeake Pottery), a circular garter with eagle in centre, used from 1879 to 1881.

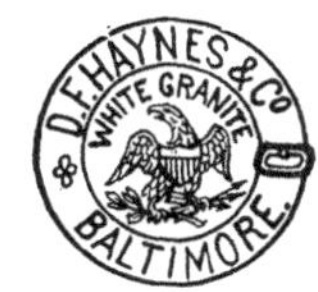


During the same period an elliptical mark with crown in centre was used on C. C. ware furnished to the same firm.

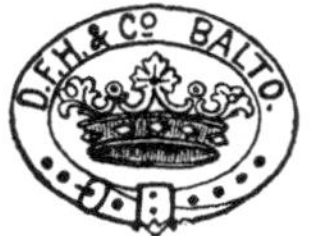


On a general line of white granite ware, from about 1881 to 1883, a circular eagle mark was used.

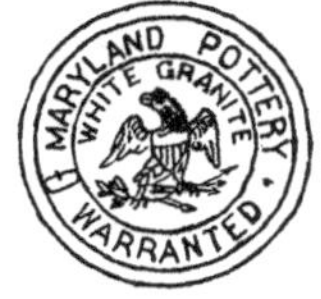


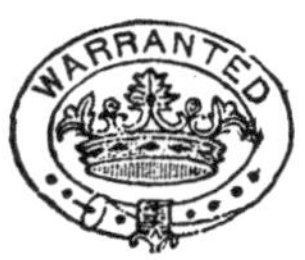


From 1880 to 1892 the crown mark was placed on their C. C. ware.

The "Cremorne" mark was used on "Opaque Porcelain" from about 1881 to 1885.

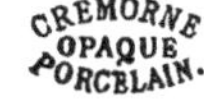


On white granite or ironstone china, between 1883 and 1891, the mark was the great Seal of the State of Maryland.

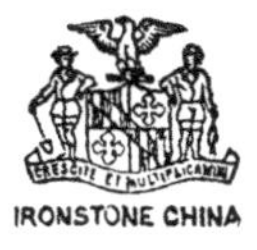


On the same ware, from 1887 to 1890, another mark was "Stone China Warranted."

STONE CHINA.
WARRANTED.

The word "Etruscan" was printed in black on a white granite toilet set from about 1885 to 1887. It was not known that a similar mark was being impressed on "Etruscan Majolica" at the Phœnixville (Pa.) Pottery about the same time.

ETRUSCAN.

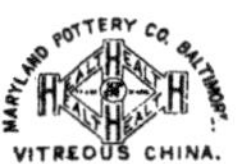


The Maryland Pottery Co. was the first to make plumbers' furnishings in "Vitreous China." Since 1891 they have been manufacturing sanitary earthenware in this body exclusively.

---

## CHESAPEAKE POTTERY, BALTIMORE, MD.

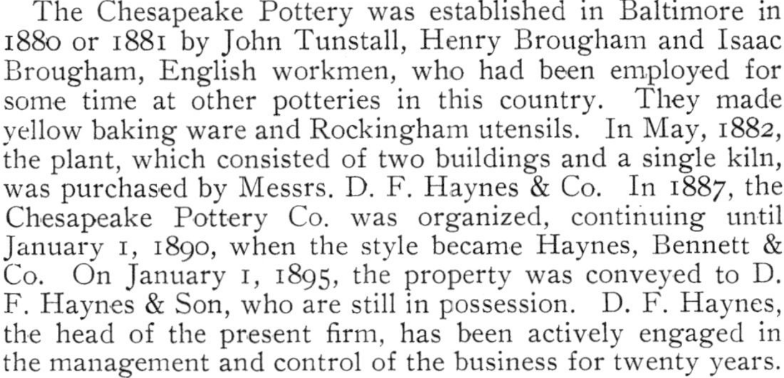
The Chesapeake Pottery was established in Baltimore in 1880 or 1881 by John Tunstall, Henry Brougham and Isaac Brougham, English workmen, who had been employed for some time at other potteries in this country. They made yellow baking ware and Rockingham utensils. In May, 1882, the plant, which consisted of two buildings and a single kiln, was purchased by Messrs. D. F. Haynes & Co. In 1887, the Chesapeake Pottery Co. was organized, continuing until January 1, 1890, when the style became Haynes, Bennett & Co. On January 1, 1895, the property was conveyed to D. F. Haynes & Son, who are still in possession. D. F. Haynes, the head of the present firm, has been actively engaged in the management and control of the business for twenty years.

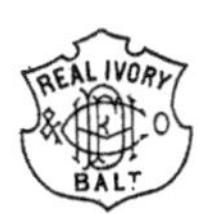


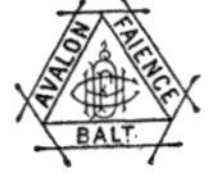


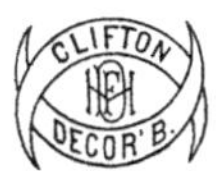


The marks used at various times at the Chesapeake Pottery are as follows:

A shield on "Ivory" body from about 1882 to 1884.

A triangular device on "Avalon" faience during the same period.

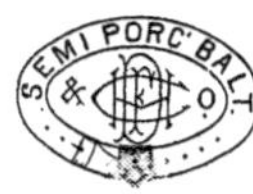


A double crescent on "Clifton" ware, with underglaze decorations and relief work, about the same time.

An ellipse on semi-porcelain during the same period.

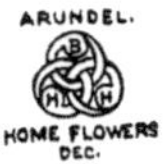


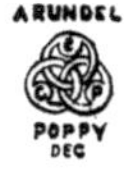


From about 1887 to 1890, or perhaps a little later, three intertwining circles were used, to indicate the shapes of dinner services, such as "Arundel," and the style of decoration, as "Home Flowers," "Poppy," "Glen Rose," "Coreopsis," etc. The letters "C. C. P." stood for Chesapeake Pottery, and "H. B. H." for Haynes & Bennett. These marks were printed on the glaze in the same colors as the overglaze decorations.

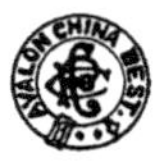


The "Avalon" mark was employed on toilet, and probably other, wares from about 1887 to 1890.

In 1900, the Haynes mark was adopted, and is used to the present time on nearly all wares that are being produced at this pottery.

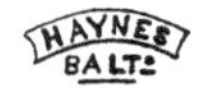


---

## MORGANTOWN, W. VA.

A pottery was established at Morgantown, W. Va., previous to 1785, which was operated after that date by James Thompson, who was succeeded by his son John W. Thompson. Later, from about 1870 to 1890, Greenland Thompson, a son of the latter, continued the manufacture.

The first product was lead-glazed red earthenware, and at a later period salt-glazed stoneware was made. The mark used on the latter was the name of the town, *impressed*. There are two varieties of this mark, one in full capitals and one in lower case letters.

MORGANTOWN

Dr. Walter Hough has directed attention to this interesting old pottery through a published report of investigations made by him in behalf of the Smithsonian Institution. At one time slip-decorated earthenware was produced at this establishment, as is shown by the large number of quill-boxes and other primitive tools which have been brought to light.

---

## WHEELING POTTERY CO., WHEELING, W. VA.

This company was organized in 1879. In 1887, a second company was formed, under the same management, known as the La Belle Pottery Co., and about two years later the two companies were consolidated. The products of the original works were white granite wares, plain and decorated, while "Adamantine" china was made at the La Belle factory. Lately a new china body, termed "Cameo" china, was introduced. This is quite thin and effectively decorated with artistic designs in various colors and in blue and gold.

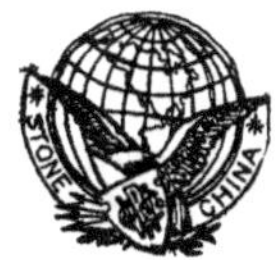


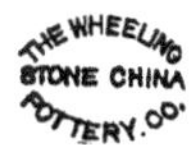

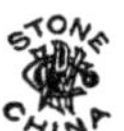


From 1880 to 1886, the first three of the marks here shown were used on white granite, and the fourth from 1886 to 1896. From the latter date to the present time the flags and eagle mark was placed on the same quality of ware.

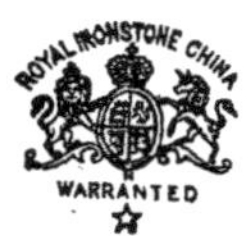


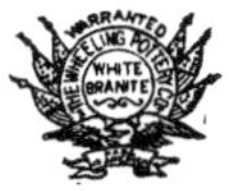


On semi-porcelain, known as "Adamantine" china, the next three marks were used from 1888 to 1893.

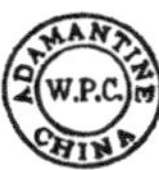


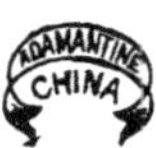


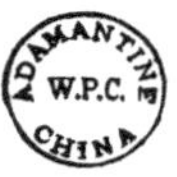


On another variety of semi-porcelain, called "La Belle" china, the two following marks were in use from 1893 to the present.

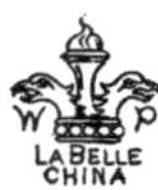


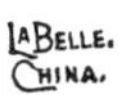


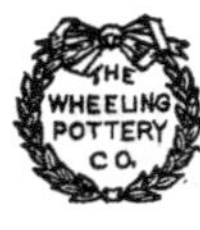


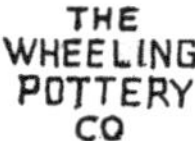


Since 1894, C. C. or cream-colored ware has been marked with a wreath enclosing the name of the company. In this body numerous souvenir designs relating to the Spanish-American war were made.

At the present time the printed name of the company is placed on "Cameo" china.

Several special stamps are yet in use by this company, of which four are here reproduced.

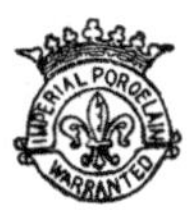

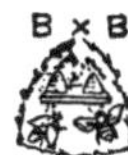


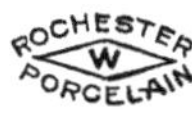


## THE WHEELING POTTERIES CO.

On January 1, 1903, the Wheeling Potteries Co. was organized by combining the Wheeling, La Belle, Riverside and Avon potteries, each of which is now a department of the former, of which Mr. Charles W. Franzheim is president and general manager. The products of these plants consist of utilitarian, sanitary and art wares. At the Wheeling and La Belle departments are produced C. C., semi-porcelain and white granite wares. Sanitary goods are made exclusively at the Riverside. At the Avon department a line of art ware is being made, decorated on the clay and burned before glazing.

The only mark used by the Avon department of the Wheeling Potteries Co. is that here shown.

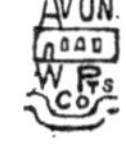


## THE OHIO VALLEY CHINA CO., WHEELING, W. VA.

This company produced a fine grade of true hard porcelain in table wares, and for a time originated some highly artistic designs in vases with perforated parts and modeled figures of cupids and eagles in high relief. The decorations and colorings were on the glaze. This pottery was closed for several years after the Chicago Exposition, but recently it has been operated under the name of the Riverside Pottery,

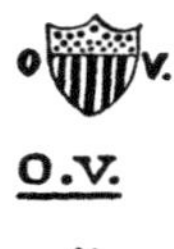


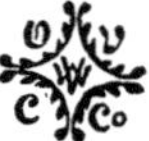

as a sanitary ware plant. The earlier mark on hotel porcelain and heavy goods was a shield in two styles, large and small, printed in green under the glaze. Later the initials of the company, O. V., were substituted. For artistic wares the mark consisted of the letters O. V. C. Co., arranged in a square, with W. V., the initials of the State, in the centre. This was printed usually in red or brown above the glaze.

---

## THE WARWICK CHINA CO., WHEELING, W. VA.

This company was organized in 1887 for the manufacture of semi-porcelain table and toilet goods. The first stamp to be used was a helmet and crossed swords, adopted about 1892, for marking novelties in semi-porcelain. From 1893 to 1898, the "Warwick Semi-Porcelain" mark was in use, and from the latter date until the present time the ware has been stamped with the name "Warwick China."

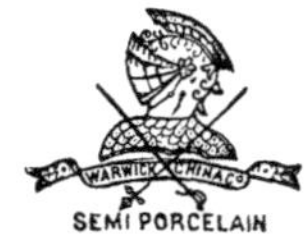


WARWICK
SEMI
PORCELAIN

WARWICK
CHINA

---

## THE VANCE FAIENCE CO., WHEELING, W. VA.

The Vance Faience Co., of Wheeling, W. Va., and Tiltonville, Ohio, recently organized, manufactures a line of art faience in colored glazes and underglaze and overglaze decorations. The mark is stamped in the green ware with a steel die.

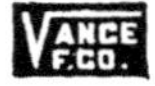


Among other specialties this company is now reproducing the hound-handled hunting pitcher, modeled by Greatbach for the old Jersey City Pottery, from the original molds.

## THE CHELSEA CHINA CO., NEW CUMBERLAND, W. VA.

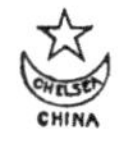


The mark used for a few years on the ware produced by this company, which was started in 1888, is a crescent and star.

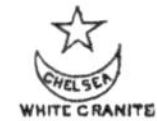


A modification of this device was used on their white granite ware at a somewhat later date.

---

## EDWARD LYCETT, ATLANTA, GA.

In 1861, Mr. Edward Lycett arrived in New York and began his long career as a decorator, after an apprenticeship of many years in some of the best establishments in England. Commencing in Green Street with only a few assistants, his business rapidly increased until his corps of decorators had reached the number of forty men and women.

In 1884, Mr. Lycett joined the New York Faience Manufacturing Co., which had established a plant at Greenpoint, Long Island. About twenty-five of the most skilful decorators were employed here, under Mr. Lycett's direction, in painting ornamental ware which surpassed everything previously produced in this country. He experimented in compounding bodies and glazes, and some of the most artistic vases produced there are entirely the work of his hands, having been designed, modeled and painted by him while the bodies and glazes are of his own composition. In 1890, he severed his connection with this company and has since been residing in Atlanta, where, in the studio of his son, William Lycett, he has been conducting experiments in lustre glazes and has demonstrated the fact that the long lost art of producing iridescent *reflects metalliques* seen in the ancient Persian tiling, can be successfully applied to our modern wares. His latest achievement is the production of an en-

E Lycett 1902

tirely new lustre, of a beautiful, deep ruby tint, and this, in combination with white enamel frosting and colored jewel work, produces most novel and pleasing effects on pure white porcelain. The mark which he uses on these productions is his name, penciled in red or gold.

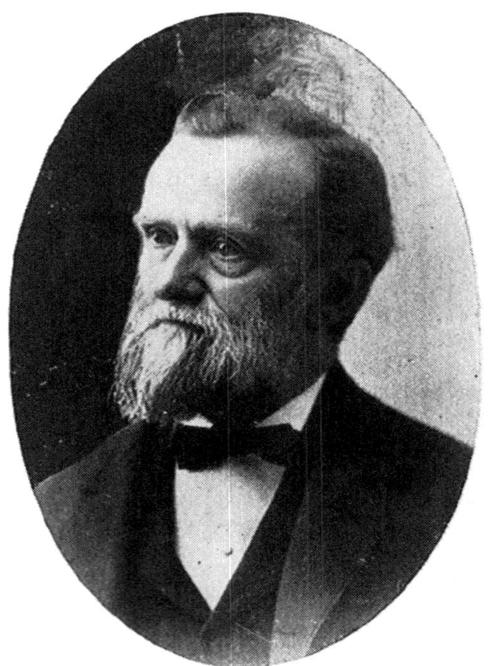

33. Edward Lycett,
The Father of China Painting in America.

Mr. Lycett is a good all-around potter, and his long and honorable career entitles him to the foremost place among china decorators in this country.

## GEORGE E. OHR, BILOXI, MISS.

Biloxi

The pottery of George E. Ohr, at Biloxi, Miss., is one of the most interesting in the United States. In a single small kiln, without assistance in the manifold labors incident to the preparation of the clay, the throwing of the pieces, the glazing and firing, Mr. Ohr has developed an original ware which has attracted the attention of the world of art. His ware is made of the ordinary clay found in the vicinity, and is burned at a low temperature. The extreme thinness of the pieces and the great variety of forms are their special characteristics. While in a plastic state they are twisted, crushed, folded, dented and crinkled into grotesque and occasionally artistic shapes, but the principal beauty of the ware consists in the richness of the glazes, which are wonderfully varied, the reds, greens and metallic lustre effects being particularly good. Being made for the most part entirely by hand, no two pieces are precisely alike. They range in size from the tiny vase or puzzle mug to pieces as tall as a man. Mr. Ohr has been potting for nearly twenty years, and all of his methods and processes are entirely original.

G. E. OHR,
BILOXI.

The marks found on the ware are the name of the potter and the town, scratched in the paste, or stamped with type.

---

## KAOLIN, S. C.

The Southern Porcelain Co., of Kaolin, S. C., manufactured Parian and fine white china to a limited extent between 1856 and 1862. They also made brown stoneware telegraph insulators. The mark on the latter, and probably on other wares, was an *impressed* shield bearing the initials of the company's name.

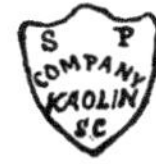

## NEWCOMB POTTERY, NEW ORLEANS, LA.

In 1896, an art department was added to the study course at Newcomb College, New Orleans, under the supervision of Prof. Ellsworth Woodward, and his assistant, Miss Mary G. Sheerer, who had studied at the Cincinnati Art Academy. The young lady pupils of the college have made great advancement in pottery designing and decoration, and some exceedingly artistic pieces have been produced there. The characteristics of the ware are original underglaze designs, suggested mainly by the local flora and fauna of the South.

In the accompanying Plate the upper figures show the factory marks. In addition to these each piece is marked with the private design or monogram of the decorator:

| | |
|---|---|
| No. 1, Leoni Nicholson. | No. 14, Elizabeth G. Rogers. |
| No. 2, Bessie A. Ficklen. | No. 15, Frances Jones. |
| No. 3, Sarah Henderson. | No. 16, Desireé Roman. |
| No. 4, Hattie Joor. | No. 17, Mary F. Baker. |
| No. 5, Gertrude R. Smith. | No. 18, Marie Hoe-LeBlane. |
| No. 6, KatherineKopman. | No. 19, Irene B. Keep. |
| No. 7, Frances H. Cocke. | No. 20, Selina E. B. Gregory. |
| No. 8, Roberta Kennon. | No. 21, Raymond A. Scudder. |
| No. 9, Mary Sheerer. | No. 22, Beverly Randolph. |
| No. 10, Mary W. Butler. | No. 23, Esther Huger Elliott. |
| No. 11, Emily Huger. | No. 24, Francis E. Lines. |
| No. 12, Amalié Roman. | No. 25, Mary W. Richardson. |
| No. 13, Mazie T. Ryan. | No. 26, Olive W. Dodd. |

No. 27, Joseph Meyers, the potter.

The letters R, U, Q, etc., indicate the clay mixtures. The letters and numbers A1, A2, etc., are the registration marks.

Recently a new decorative treatment has been introduced, the outlining of conventionalized designs by means of a pointed instrument, in the *art nouveau* style.

The products of the Newcomb Pottery have taken such a prominent place in the art world that possessors of examples of this ware will be glad to be able to identify the work of the various artists who have placed their marks on them.

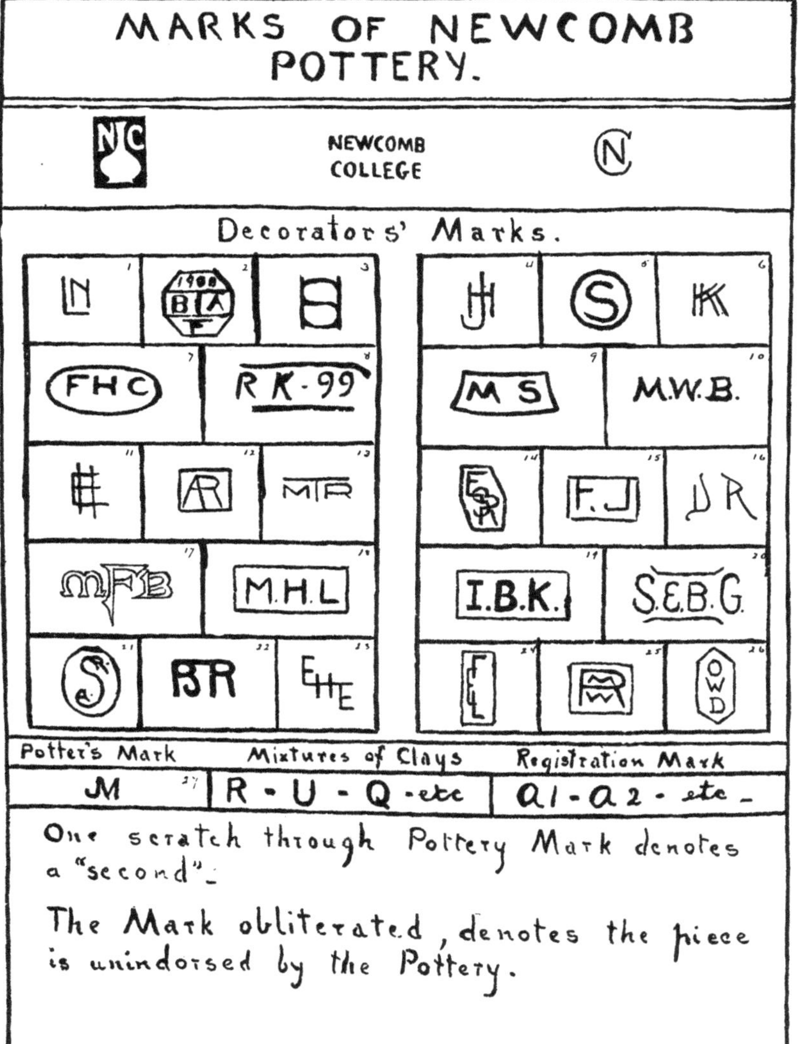
MARKS OF NEWCOMB POTTERY.
NEWCOMB COLLEGE
Decorators' Marks.
FHC
RK-99
MS
M.W.B.
M.H.L
I.B.K.
S.E.B.G.
Potter's Mark
Mixtures of Clays
Registration Mark
JM
R - U - Q - etc
a1 - a2 - etc -
One scratch through Pottery Mark denotes a "second".
The Mark obliterated, denotes the piece is unindorsed by the Pottery.

# POTTERIES
# OF THE WESTERN STATES

---

# WESTERN STATES.

## THE PEORIA POTTERY CO., PEORIA, ILL.

THE Peoria Pottery Co. was organized in 1873. The original buildings were erected in 1859 by Messrs. C. W. Fenton and D. W. Clark, who had previously been connected with the United States Pottery at Bennington, Vt. Mr. Fenton was the president of the corporation which was named the American Pottery Co. The mark first used was a circular, impressed stamp bearing the name of the company around the margin and "Peoria, Ill." in the centre. After making white granite and C. C. wares for about three years the works were taken by other parties, who began the manufacture of yellow, Rockingham and stoneware. In 1867 and 1868, the mark for yellow ware was the name of the pottery *impressed*. The same mark was used on brown glazed (Albany slip) stoneware from 1867 to 1887.

PEORIA
ILLINOIS

The later marks of the Peoria Pottery Co. are as follows:

On C. C. ware, from 1888 to 1890, the British Coat of Arms. These marks were used temporarily, when changing from stoneware to whiteware.

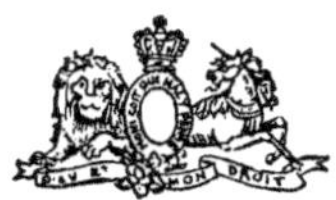

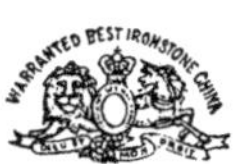

On C. C. ware, from 1890 to 1899 (when this product was abandoned), the monogram of the company's name was used.

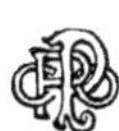

On white granite, from 1890 to the present time, the British Arms again served as a mark, and during the same period the monogram was used on semi-porcelain.

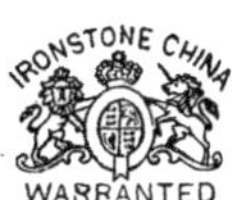


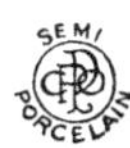


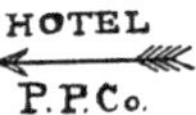


In 1889 and 1890, the mark on C. C. hotel ware was an arrow. All of these are printed in black (see also the Crown Pottery Co.).

---

## THE AMERICAN TERRA-COTTA CO., CHICAGO, ILL.

TECO

The American Terra-Cotta and Ceramic Co. have recently placed upon the market a new product, which is known as Teco ware. It is made in plain shapes, usually with modeled or relief designs, covered with a dull or matt glaze of a peculiar grayish-green tint. It is stamped with the word "Teco," derived from the title of the company.

---

## THE MONMOUTH POTTERY CO., MONMOUTH, ILL.

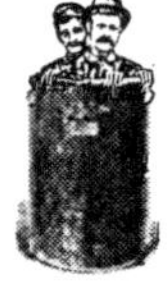

The products of this factory are all kinds of stoneware. The mark represents an enormous vessel containing two men. The numbers indicate the different sizes of the ware.

## THE CROWN POTTERY CO., EVANSVILLE, IND.

The Crown Pottery Co. began operations on October 1, 1891, with six kilns and four enamel kilns. The products are white granite table and toilet wares. The marks are as follows:

On ironstone china.

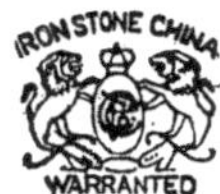


On "Crown Porcelain" dinner ware.

*Crown Porcelain.*

On dinner ware, the crown mark.

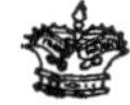

On various patterns of dinner ware,—"Rex," "Regina," "Royal" and "Jewel":

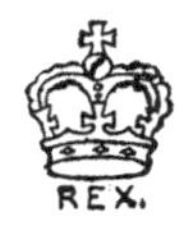


| C. P. CO. REX | REGINA C. P. CO. | C. P. CO. ROYAL | JEWEL C.P.Co. |
|---|---|---|---|

On toilet ware patterns,—"Alma," "Helen," "Hobson" and "Rena":

ALMA HELEN. HOBSON RENA.

On semi-porcelain.

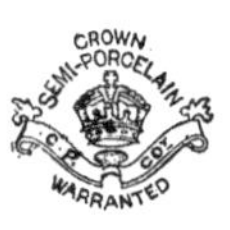


On hotel ware.

CROWN HOTEL WARE.

This pottery dates back to 1882, when it was established by A. M. Beck. He began the manufacture of majolica with three kilns. In 1884, at Mr. Beck's death, the works were taken by Bennighof, Uhl & Co., who began the manufacture of white ware.

Recently the Crown Pottery Co. and the Peoria Pottery Co., of Peoria, Ill., have been combined as the Crown Potteries Co.

---

## THE PAULINE POTTERY CO., EDGERTON, WIS.

The Pauline Pottery Co. made underglaze decorated art wares from 1888 to some time about 1894. This pottery was originally established by Mrs. Pauline Jacobus in Chicago, in 1883. The mark, impressed in the earlier pieces and printed in black on the later, consisted of a crown with the letter C, for Chicago.

---

## MRS. S. S. FRACKELTON, MILWAUKEE, WIS.

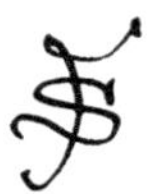

Mrs. S. S. Frackelton, of Milwaukee, Wis., is widely known for her artistic creations in common salt-glazed stoneware, and the mark which she uses on her work is composed of the initials of her name.

---

## THE STOCKTON ART POTTERY CO., STOCKTON, CAL.

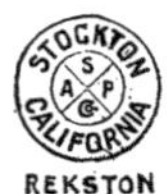


The Stockton Art Pottery Co. was incorporated a few years ago, at Stockton, Cal. The principal products were jardinières and pedestals, umbrella stands and vases. The special art ware, which was christened "Rekston" ware, is characterized by heavy, colored glazes or enamels. The company was originally called the Stockton Terra-Cotta Co., and the word "Rekston," originally spelled "Reckston," was obtained by taking the words "Stockton Terra-Cotta" and eliminating the duplicate letters and using those which remained, with the exception of the letter "a." Later the "c" was omitted, leaving the name as shown in their mark,

"Rekston." We are unable to state whether this company is still in existence, as repeated letters of inquiry have remained unanswered. The mark is *impressed.*

---

## THE GEIJSBEEK POTTERY CO., GOLDEN, COL.

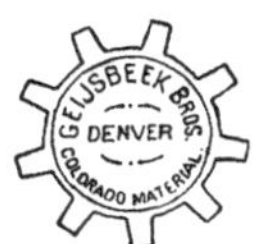


This company began operations in 1899. From September of that year until February, 1900, the marks used on white ware and vitrified colored bodies were "The Geijsbeek Pottery Co., Denver, Colo.," and the initials "G. P. C." From February to August, 1900, their mark was a wheel with spokes and the word "Denver" in the centre, *printed* in black.

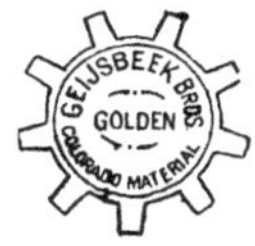


From the latter date until January, 1901, the same mark, with the name "Golden" in the centre, was in use.

This was superseded, at the beginning of the last-named year, by a similar mark, on white ware, printed in green beneath the glaze.

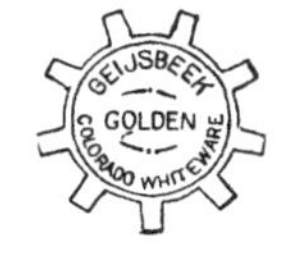


The products of this company are made from Colorado clays.

---

## THE DENVER CHINA AND POTTERY CO.

The Denver China and Pottery Co. was recently organized in Denver, Col., by Dr. W. A. Long, who is president of the new company. Lonhuda ware is again being made and decorated by some of the old artists who were employed by the Lonhuda Co., in Zanesville. A new line of art ware, known by the name of "Denaura," in matt glazes of various colors, principally green, has been developed. The surface is sometimes iridescent, showing flits of rich metallic, prismatic coloring. The pieces are modeled with relief designs of native Colorado flowers, with lines and motives in Art Nouveau style.

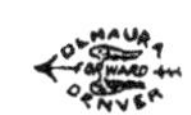


This company also manufactures a new line of general ware, for ordinary uses, and colored glazed wares.

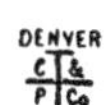

## SAN FRANCISCO, CAL.

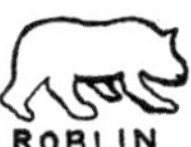


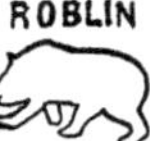


An art pottery was established in San Francisco, Cal., by Mrs. Linna Irelan, about 1899. Her designs are modeled from nature and all the pieces are thrown on the wheel. The native clays of California are used exclusively. Mr. Alexander W. Robertson, formerly of Chelsea, Mass., assists her in creating artistic shapes. The colored glazes or enamels which are used are especially meritorious. The decorations are incised and in relief. Mrs. Irelan has given this pottery the name of Roblin ware, which is formed from the first syllables of Mr. Robertson's name and her Christian name.

The mark is the word "Roblin," in conjunction with the figure of a bear, *impressed* in the clay. In addition to this device are usually found the name of the designer and certain numbers or characters relating to the records of the establishment.

---

## THE VAN BRIGGLE POTTERY CO., COLORADO SPRINGS, COL.

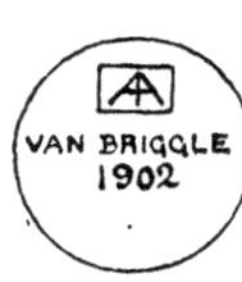


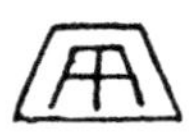

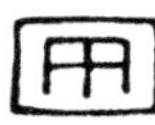

The Van Briggle Pottery Co. was organized at Colorado Springs, Col., in 1901, by Artus Van Briggle, formerly a decorator at the Rookwood Pottery, in Cincinnati. The founder spent three years in Paris, where he studied drawing and the human figure. The product of this, one of the most recent American art potteries, is characterized by originality of treatment in the modeled ornamentation and a peculiar soft, dull glaze. The designs are modeled in relief before the ware is fired. The details of the human figures are often suggestive, as though emerging from water, the effect being most artistic. In some of the simpler pieces the decoration is a conventionalized treatment of geometrical and floral devices. The mark, which is incised in the clay with a blunt tool, consists of a monogram, the name of the projector and the date, the latter being changed each year.

Variations of this mark occur on vases of a high artistic

quality. The "dead" glaze is of a fine, smooth texture, and is produced in a variety of tints.

Mr. Van Briggle died at Colorado Springs in the summer of 1904.

---

## DETROIT, MICH.

An art pottery, original in conception and treatment, has been perfected by Miss Mary Chase Perry, at Detroit, Mich. This pottery, which has been called Pewabic ware, after the northern river of that name, is of hard, white body covered with heavy opaque enamels of various colors, coming from the kiln with a natural matt finish which is most pleasing to the sight and touch. The forms of the ware are simple and graceful; the ornamentation is usually in relief, consisting of natural and conventional leaf forms artistically and harmoniously modeled. Some of the pieces appear in monochrome, the color scheme running through the greens, purples and yellows. Other examples exhibit pleasing combinations of flow glazes in various shades of yellow and brown or in blue, purple and white. One of the most pleasing and novel effects is produced by crystalline spots of a light shade which are scattered evenly through a uniform ground color. While the dull green enamel possesses a tone quality entirely different from that of any other ware, it is in the orange yellow, streaked with warm, rich browns that Miss Perry has achieved her greatest success. In some of the pieces the heavy enamel of one or more shades trickles down the sides on a ground of a different tint, suggestive of some of the slow flowing glazes of Oriental wares.

One important feature of this manufacture is the method of firing the ware, which is done in the open flame of a muffle kiln without the use of saggers, kerosene oil being the fuel which has been found possible to produce this result. The pottery has been equipped with an electric plant by means of which the machinery is operated.

PEWABIC

M C P

The mark, which is *impressed* in the ware, consists of the name PEWABIC, beneath a row of leaves. On some of the pieces also occur the letters M. C. P., the initials of the maker, Miss Mary C. Perry.

# INDEX.

www.ingramcontent.com/pod-product-compliance
Lightning Source LLC
LaVergne TN
LVHW010100110826
845155LV00028B/416

* 9 7 8 1 9 3 0 6 6 5 4 1 5 *